GIVING AND
GENEROSITY

[Giving and Tithing
Generosity and Benevolence]

MONEYLIFE™ BASICS SERIES

ISBN 978-1-56427-256-0

Verses identified as (NIV) are taken from the *Holy Bible: New International Version*, ©1973, 1978, 1984 by the International Bible Society. Used by permission of Zondervan Bible Publishers.

Verses identified as (TLB) are taken from *The Living Bible*, ©1971 by Tyndale House Publishers, Wheaton, Illinois. Used by permission.

All other Scripture quotations are taken from the *New American Standard Bible*® (Updated Edition) (NASB), ©1960, 1962, 1963, 1968, 1971, 1972, 1973, 1975, 1977, 1995 by The Lockman Foundation. Used by permission.

MoneyLife™ is a trademark of Crown Financial Ministries.

For inquiries in Canada, please contact CrownCanada.ca or call 1-866-401-0626.

September 2008 Edition

CONTENTS

INTRODUCTION

This book's first two chapters deal with giving and tithing are important and somewhat controversial subjects. No one objects to the idea that followers of Christ should be generous givers; the controversy comes when we attempt to define details. Sometimes the detailed discussion appears to move in a direction that feels more like law than grace. That is never our intent.

When we consider Old Testament sources or quote Mosaic law, it is not to resurrect a legalistic approach to giving. Rather, it is to further our understanding of God's heart in providing the law to begin with. Any legalistic attitude in our giving would defeat our desire to please Him.

Imagine standing face to face with God with the goal of discovering His will for what you should give. Imagine asking the question, "What specifically do you want from me?"

His answer to you might differ from His answer to anyone else. It would probably depend on what you value, but from His perspective the meaning is always the same: "Give me your heart."

God knows He can have your obedience without your heart, but that brings Him no pleasure. Jesus drove that point by identifying the greatest commandment of all: "Love the Lord your God with all your heart and with all your soul and with all your mind."

This kind of love requires our trust, which is why God pleads over and over throughout Scripture for us to trust Him. As we discuss giving and tithing, we must never lose sight of God's perspective—what He values. Our goal is to please Him in everything, including our giving.

The third chapter of this book deals with generosity and benevolence, a practical response to the physical needs of people around us. You have probably given directly to someone in need. It may have been an isolated incident or it may have led to additional involvement. At some point, you may have felt some concern over questions like these:

- What is the best way to help?
- Could my help actually hurt more than help?
- What if the need is bigger than my available resources?
- What if the need is ongoing?

- What if the person requires emotional/spiritual help?

Many needs require help beyond what any one of us can give. In designing the Church as the body of Christ, God supplied its members with a variety of gifts to be used in a coordinated fashion. Together we can do what none of us can do alone.

We will always have poor people who, for various reasons, are incapable of meeting their own needs. For some, the incapacity is short-term. For others, it may be lifelong. Regardless of the need, God cares about them and has clearly called us to care about them as well.

Many churches and individuals have taken this call seriously and, in the process, have discovered rich opportunities for service and ministry. Many of their members had felt frustration—even guilt—over needs that seemed beyond their ability to meet until someone began to organize volunteers and match their skills with people's needs.

Such ministry efforts may adopt a variety of names, but we use the generic label "Benevolence" to identify them. Chapter 2 of this book will give you a vision for what can be done. It may even open a door for your personal involvement.

This book will help you if you:

- wonder what the Bible teaches about giving and tithing,

- want encouragement in your desire to give,

- want to learn practical ways to personally help others through acts of kindness,

- want to help your church start or improve its Benevolence ministry, or

- want to make sure you don't miss one of the greatest blessings God offers.

    You may be in financial need and feel unable to give as generously as you would like. There is hope for you. God knows your heart. He isn't concerned for what you cannot do; He is concerned about unclaimed blessings that result from what you are unwilling to do. When you determine to trust God—and to grow in your trust—your heart pleases Him far beyond any large monetary gift you don't have. Remember that God is the owner of all of your possessions as you consider what you believe in your heart He is leading you to do. When He leads, He also empowers. You can do it!

Help and Hope Are Here.

Crown exists to provide help, hope, and insight. These Help and Hope buttons appear whenever special information is available to assist and encourage you.

Please notice a few helpful features we include in every *MoneyLife™ Basics Series* book.

1. Appendix 1 is an introduction to Christ. If you (or someone you know) are uncertain about where you stand with God, this short introduction will guide you into an intimate relationship with Him.

2. Appendix 2, "God's Ownership & Financial Faithfulness," briefly explores a fundamental concept—one that frames the correct perspective on every financial principle in Scripture. If you don't understand this, you are likely to manage your resources with worldly wisdom. The world's approach to money management isn't always evil, but it is short-sighted (ignoring eternity), incomplete (ignoring the Creator/Controller/Provider), and usually in pursuit of the wrong goals.

3. Because we are committed to transformation rather than mere information, each chapter ends with a two-part exercise:

   - An Action Step you create based on your response to the chapter

     - A Celebration Plan for every Action Step completed

       Please take advantage of these to become a doer rather than just a hearer. *"Do not merely listen to the word, and so deceive yourselves. Do what it says"* (James 1:22, NIV).

CHAPTER 1

GIVING AND TITHING

Section 1: Tithing

Begging to Give

In the Bible, the eighth chapter of 2 Corinthians provides a powerful account of giving. Poverty was no stranger to the first century church at Macedonia, yet their generosity was so great that it continues to be a model for giving almost 2,000 years later. The source of their generosity was in their *spiritual* wealth, which overflowed in such abundant giving that the apostle Paul made note of it repeatedly in his epistles.

Paul says the Macedonians were pleased to give, and God loves a cheerful giver. They gave *of their own accord*, not grudgingly or under compulsion. They *begged* Paul for the opportunity to give, not having to be begged themselves. And they entreated Paul for the favor of helping support the saints. For them, giving was a privilege.

More than anything, however, giving seemed to be a natural response to the Macedonians. It is that type of giving that is done in love, requires no audience, and is followed by no reasoning or regrets. It springs from a deep spiritual relationship that puts God in the proper perspective: as owner of all things.

Psalms 24:1 declares, *"The earth is the Lord's, and all it contains."* Deuteronomy 8:18 says it is God who gives us power to make wealth, not we ourselves. And in 1 Corinthians 4:7, Paul asks *"What do you have that you did not receive?"*

When we recognize that God owns everything and all blessings come from Him (including our ability to work), our role as managers, or stewards, becomes evident. We can see and experience the multitude of blessings we have to be thankful for.

In response, we should view ourselves as God's servants, ready always to do His will. That is why we call Him Lord, meaning "ruler," "owner," "sovereign," "king." God is good, faithful, and generous. It is a privilege to trust Him and recognize Him as owner!

Who's in Charge?

When we view ourselves as owners rather than managers, we tend to look at every other aspect of our lives the same way. We see ourselves as being in charge, but that changes quickly in the face of circumstances beyond our control.

In our coaching sessions at Crown, we have met several people who had learned that they had terminal illnesses. The news instantly changed their perspective on the future and material things; they no longer looked at this world as their measure of value.

Too often we find ourselves distracted by buildings, cars, investments, and retirement plans for 30 years in the future. The very second we cease to breathe, all of these concerns will be irrelevant.

The Bible story of Job is another reminder that no one has a permanent hold on anything in this world, no matter how powerful he or she is. Suddenly stripped of his many possessions, Job confirmed this fact, pointing to his own mortality as the undeniable evidence of God's controlling ownership: *"Naked I came from my mother's womb, and naked I shall return there. The Lord gave and the Lord has taken away"* (Job 1:21).

Money is not ours; it is God's, given to us to hold in trust and manage for His purposes. He allots different amounts to His children, based on His plan and purpose for their lives. And someday we'll be held accountable for the way we managed our allotments. God wants us to succeed, to have our family's needs met, and to be generous givers. He can equip us to do it all.

How Much Should We Give?

Part of being a good manager, or steward, is giving back to God a portion of what He's entrusted to us. It's not that God "needs" our money. Rather, giving serves as an external, material testimony that God owns both the material and spiritual things of our lives. It also supports the greatest, most enduring work ever conducted in this world: God's work.

One of the first standards of giving found in the Bible is the tithe, a word which means "tenth." Abraham tithed in Genesis 14 after returning from the daring rescue of his nephew Lot from four enemy kings. He encountered the priest Melchizedek and voluntarily surrendered to him one-tenth of all the spoils he had taken from his enemies. It's often said that the tithe is Old Testament legalism, but Abraham tithed some 430 years before the Law was given to Moses.

The Storehouse

"'Bring the whole tithe into the storehouse, so that there may be food in My house…'" (Malachi 3:10).

In order to bring our tithes into the storehouse, it is necessary to determine exactly what the storehouse is. In biblical times it was a physical place where the Jews would deliver their offerings of grain or animals. A storehouse had specific functions according to God's Word.

- *To feed the tribe of Levi* (Numbers 18:24-29). The tribe of Levi and the priests would be equivalent to pastors and other church staff, missionaries, and evangelists.

- *To feed the Hebrew widows and orphans living within the Hebrew city* (Deuteronomy 14:28-29). They would be equivalent to the widows and orphans served in a local church.

- *To feed the Gentile poor living in the Hebrew city* (Deuteronomy 14:28-29). Today's equivalent would be unchurched needy people in the community surrounding a local church.

Ideally, the local church could serve as the storehouse in God's economy today. Then people's tithes would simply be given to the church. After all, God has designed the church to carry out vital social functions among Christians and non-Christians, as shown above.

These functions also include ministering to the sick, teaching families to care for themselves, and taking the gospel to the lost at home and abroad. Unfortunately, the vast majority of local churches do not minister fully in these areas.

Therefore, to the extent that a church lacks in a specific area of ministry, a portion of the tithe may be given to the individual or para-church organization that is "filling in the gap." But remember that you should not sit under the teaching of a local church without supporting it financially (1 Timothy 5:17-18).

If you see areas of ministry that you think your church is not addressing, share your concerns with the church leadership in an open, loving manner. If there is no response, prayerfully consider whether this is the church that God wants you to attend. God knows your heart and has a place for you where you can worship and serve in your community.

Learning to Fear God

During Moses' time, the tithe was established so that the children of Israel might learn to fear God.

Deuteronomy 14:22-23 says, *"You shall surely tithe all the produce from what you sow, which comes out of the field every year. You shall eat in the presence of the Lord your God, at the place where He chooses to establish His name, the tithe of your grain, your new wine, your oil, and the firstborn of your herd and your flock,* **so that you may learn to fear the Lord your God always"** (emphasis added).

But what about the implications of this statement today? Does it still apply to God's people? Psalm 111:10 says, *"The fear of the Lord is the beginning of wisdom."* If we want to be wise in handling our finances, we must seek wisdom from God. One of the ways God intends for us to do this is to acknowledge His Lordship by tithing to Him.

When we don't fear God, we discount His Lordship and put our will ahead of His, losing our eternal perspective and allowing temporary worldly things to gain importance. We allow money and possessions to become our gods just as surely as the Israelites abandoned God to worship idols before the captivity.

The result for Israel was bondage in a foreign land. For us, it's bondage to stuff, which often leads to debt, stress, divorce and ruined lives. Striving after stuff also diverts us from the fulfillment of eternal accomplishment.

"For no man can lay a foundation other than the one which is laid, which is Jesus Christ. Now if any man builds on the foundation with gold, silver, precious stones, wood, hay, straw, each man's work will become evident; for the day will show it because it is to be revealed with fire, and the fire itself will test the quality of each man's work. If any man's work which he has built on it remains, he will receive a reward. If any man's work is burned up, he will suffer loss; but he himself will be saved, yet so as through fire" (1 Corinthians 3:11-15).

Imagine staring into eternity with nothing to show for our time here on earth. The length of this life and the things we substituted for God would be pathetically apparent. Thankfully, life gives us a daily opportunity to make God our central desire and take steps to become generous givers.

When Spouses Disagree

Tithing, like any other financial issue, can be a source of controversy between a husband and wife. When both are followers of Christ, they should share a desire to honor God with their priorities and financial management.

It's important for both spouses to understand what God says about money. When they do, they'll understand that tithing is God-ordained, not just a personal desire that the wife is trying to impose on the husband or vice versa.

The problem becomes more complicated when one spouse is an unbeliever. If the unbelieving spouse is the husband, then the believing wife should submit to his wishes, trusting that her submissive attitude may win him to the Lord. *"…you wives, be submissive to your own husbands so that even if any of them are disobedient to the word, they may be won without a word by the behavior of their wives"* (1 Peter 3:1-6).

We recommend that she consider asking him to try an experiment for a year. During that time, he would allow her to give an amount acceptable to him (probably smaller than the tithe) for at least a year. If at the end of a year they are worse off financially as a result of her giving, she agrees to stop. But if they are better off, she will be allowed to give more.

"'Bring the whole tithe into the storehouse, so that there may be food in My house, and test Me now in this,' says the LORD of hosts, 'if I will not open for you the windows of heaven and pour out for you a blessing until it overflows'" (Malachi 3:10).

The Lord says to test Him in tithing. This gives God an opportunity to prove Himself to an unbelieving spouse.

When the roles are reversed and the wife is the unbeliever, the husband, in obeying God's direction, should realize that God is more concerned about his wife's soul than his money. If tithing becomes a stumbling block to his wife, he should consider not tithing temporarily out of respect for her wishes. The thought behind this is that she might be won in the same way Peter describes. And, of course, she may also be open to the experiment we described.

During this time, God sees the genuine desire of the spouse who wants to tithe and understands any relational limitations in the marriage. He can be trusted to work out the details.

Is the Tithe a Limit?

One excuse for not tithing is that it limits the amount a follower of Christ gives to God. But the tithe was never meant to be a limit. In fact, the Jews were admonished to give nearly one-fourth of their income each year.

With such giving today, the church could replace government welfare programs. But most people need a starting point. We can find no record of God ever asking less than a tenth from anyone. But if 10 percent seems like a tip rather than an expression of loving dependence, give 11 percent, 12 percent, or as much as you desire. Some have fulfilled their personal goals to give 90 percent!

Living under grace means we're not compelled to do anything by virtue of a

written law. Grace is unmerited and un-
earned favor, not a license to do nothing.
God's desire is that we give with joy rather
than obligation. *"Each one must do just as
he has purposed in his heart, not grudgingly
or under compulsion, for God loves a cheerful
giver"* (2 Corinthians 9:7).

Again, the principle of God's ownership comes into play. God
doesn't own just 10 percent of our money, he owns 100 percent. That's why we should never tithe with the view that the
remainder is ours.

After giving our tithe, God may impress us to give an additional
amount to a missionary, rescue mission, or other work. (Gen-
eral guidelines for all types of giving, including that which goes
beyond the tithe, are covered in the next section.)

Jess and Angie Correll's Giving Transformation

WHEN JESS CORRELL WAS 19 and his brother
was 17, they made it their goal to become the
richest men in Kentucky. Remembering their
goal through the years to become rich, the Correll brothers "pursued it with a vengeance," Jess says. "We
acquired a financially struggling company every two years and
kept building our wealth."

However, success came at a price, and Jess' marriage ended
in divorce. "I worked too hard," he says, "and I was too single-
minded and focused.

Today, Jess realizes that when it came to money, he didn't

have a proper perspective—God's perspective. At the encouragement of a friend, Jess and the top five officers in his banking company went through a Crown small group study. At the time, Jess and his brother were about $20 million in debt.

After completing the Crown study, the brothers made a commitment to stop expanding, get control of their spending, and start paying down their debt. They became debt free in only five years, and if they incur any debt today, it is only short term.

During the years they were living at home, Jess and his brother watched their father faithfully tithe. They also tithed based on their after-tax income, but as they paid off their debt, they began tithing based on their pre-tax income and have been doing so ever since. Jess says giving has been fun since he learned God's financial principles, and today he gives a large percentage of his income beyond the tithe. In addition, the Correll's banking company has a foundation that gives away 10 percent of pre-tax earnings—a key advantage of being debt free.

Following his divorce, Jess remained single for five years before marrying his wife, Angela. He views her as a gift from

God and likens her to the example of a good wife in Proverbs 31:10, *"An excellent wife, who can find? For her worth is far above jewels."*

"She is an absolute partner in every way," he says. "She's my closest adviser, and we don't make significant giving decisions without each other's opinion. Most of the time we pray individually about how much to give to a particular organization, and generally, we come up with the same amount to give. It's a confirmation of who we should be supporting and how much we should be giving them."

Just as he benefited from Crown, Jess wants to see others receive the same benefits. For that reason, he has become active in Crown by sharing its teachings with his family, by serving on the ministry's board of directors, and by funding its work.

"Crown is the number one ministry that our foundation supports. Investing in Crown is like buying Microsoft 10 years ago for a penny a share. It's an excellent investment with a huge impact."

Answers to Questions about Tithing

- *When I calculate my tithe, should it be on my net or my gross income?* Proverbs 3:9-10 says that God has asked for our firstfruits, which is the first and best of all that we receive. We interpret this to be our total personal income before taxes (gross).

  - *Should I tithe if I am in debt?* As already discussed, the tithe helps us to fear God, which is the beginning of wisdom. If there is anyone in the world who needs God's wisdom in the area of finances, it is a person who is already in debt.

- *Is it okay to take my tithe money and put it toward Bible college tuition?* Malachi 3 says we are actually stealing from God if we don't pay an honest tithe. Saving for a Christian education is a good thing, but not if our lack of trust causes us to rob God for it.

- *Could tithe money be used to support secular organiza-*

tions? The tithe is given in God's name and should be used specifically for His work.

- *Should I tithe from the profits of the sale of my house?* Any profit from any sale should be tithed, because it is, in fact, part of our firstfruits. Even if the profits are to be reinvested in a new home, a tithe should be given first. Remember, it was God who enabled us to realize the profit.

- *Should a person tithe on an inheritance?* Yes. An inheritance is part of our "increase."

- *What about insurance payments received after the death of a spouse—should a person tithe on the lump sum or just on the interest earnings?* Again, look at the principle of tithing on our "increase." If insurance proceeds are paid in a lump sum distribution, a tithe should first be paid on the entire amount.

  1. Afterward a tithe should be paid on any increase received (interest, dividends or growth) from the investment of those funds.

  2. If rather than being paid in a lump sum, the proceeds are held in trust and distributed periodically, then a tithe should be paid on each distribution.

- *If my parents are in great need, can I give a part of my tithe money to help them?* In Matthew 15:5-6 Jesus condemns the Pharisees' practice of consecrating their possessions to God while their parents suffered need.

  In light of this, if the tithe is the only resource available to help our parents, we can give it to them. However, we should be sure we have sacrificed our discretionary funds before giving what belongs to God.

- *Should I tithe on alimony or child support from my ex-husband?* Alimony is income from which a tithe should be given, but child support belongs to the children and isn't part of personal "increase."

- *Wouldn't you be exempt from tithing if you were on a fixed income (Social Security, pension, annuity) and barely making ends meet?* As already stated, God doesn't "need" our money. His desire is to bless His children, and it is for our good that He has instituted the principle of tithing in His Word.

Remember the widow who put two "mites" into the treasury? Jesus knew her situation and commended her by saying, *"This poor widow put in more than all the contributors to the treasury; for they all put in out of their surplus, but she, out of her poverty, put in all she owned, all she had to live on"* (Mark 12:43-44).

Giving with the Right Attitude

As with all of our service, giving (including the tithe) should be done with the right attitude. When giving is viewed as a rule and done out of a sense of duty, it becomes legalism.

Giving is never legalistic when we do it in thanksgiving to God. A few moments spent counting our blessings always reminds us of reasons to be thankful, including our ability to work.

Giving in the hope that we'll receive two or three times as much is also a wrong attitude. Romans 11:35 says, *"Or who has first given to Him that it might be paid back to Him again?"* If we give only to receive, then we are no better than Simon, described in Acts 8, who offered money to the apostles in hopes of receiving spiritual power.

His offer brought a stern rebuke from Peter, who answered, *"May your silver perish with you, because you thought you could obtain the gift of God with money!"* (Acts 8:20).

Another wrong attitude is giving out of fear. Reverence and respect toward God, when tempered with confidence in His love, are signs of spiritual maturity. This is a healthy kind of fear, as noted earlier in Psalm 111:10 and repeated in Proverbs 9:10: *"The fear of the Lord is the beginning of wisdom."* Our giving should not be out of fear that God will punish us if we don't give.

If we give because we feel intimidated, then we are giving under compulsion, which is contrary to 2 Corinthians 9:7. Never support a ministry that uses threats as a fundraising gimmick.

Finally, we should never give to impress others. In Matthew 6:2-4, Jesus gave us the following warning: *"So when you give to the poor, do not sound a trumpet before you, as the hypocrites do in the synagogues and in the streets, so that they may be honored by men. Truly I say to you, they have their reward in full. But when you give to the poor, do not let your left hand know what your right hand is doing, so that your giving will be in secret; and your Father who sees what is done in*

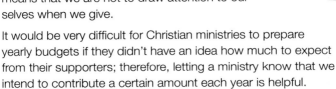

secret will reward you."

People who have a problem with pride need to do their giving in a modest and humble way. This doesn't mean that all giving must be done entirely in secret. It simply means that we are not to draw attention to ourselves when we give.

It would be very difficult for Christian ministries to prepare yearly budgets if they didn't have an idea how much to expect from their supporters; therefore, letting a ministry know that we intend to contribute a certain amount each year is helpful.

Allowing our children to witness our giving, particularly when sacrifice is involved, teaches them the importance of commitment. Giving for applause or approval from others, however, is unscriptural. Our greatest satisfaction is God's overflowing joy when we give generously as He does.

Section 2: Giving Beyond the Tithe

Reasons for Giving

Like tithing, giving beyond the tithe should be an outward material expression of a deeper spiritual commitment and an indication of a willing and obedient heart.

We should give as the Macedonians did, out of a grateful heart and with an attitude of joy. The cheerful giving principle of 2 Corinthians 9:7 applies to all giving, especially as increasingly large amounts of money are given.

Another reason for giving beyond the tithe is conviction. Perhaps the Holy Spirit is prompting you to give to a special cause. How can you determine if such a desire to give is actually from God or just an emotional response? Read God's Word and pray. If you are married, include your spouse in the decision to ensure balance in your giving.

Finally, some may have the spiritual gift of giving described by the apostle Paul in Romans 12:8: *"he who gives, with liberality."* These people live very disciplined lives, enabling them to give generously. They are especially sensitive to the needs of others and conscious of the need to check out every cause they give to. Generally, they are very prudent people.

How to Give

When giving beyond the tithe, we should give out of our abundance according to the principle taught in 2 Corinthians 8:14 At the present time your plenty will supply what they need, so that in turn their plenty will supply what you need. Then there will be equality *"God doesn't want us to give until we are made poor unless it is to improve our lives spiritually"*. Proverbs 30:8-9 presents a balanced attitude toward material things. *"Give me neither poverty nor riches; Feed me with the food that is my portion, that I not be full and deny You and say, 'Who is the LORD?' Or that I not be in want and steal, and profane the name of my God."*

God's main concern is what is in our hearts. Other guidelines for this type of giving include the following.

- *Knowing the difference between faith promises and pledges—*

    1. A faith promise is a commitment to give a certain amount, which allows ministries to prepare a good financial

plan for the year. It is under-
stood that if God doesn't
provide the funds, we're not
obligated to give them.

2. A pledge, on the other hand, is
a commitment to pay something.
This type of giving can be like debt—
presuming on the future—whereas a faith promise
is conditionaed on God's provision. *"Now faith is
the assurance of things hoped for, the conviction
of things not seen"* (Hebrews 11:1).

- *Donating something other than money—*

  1. We may donate time or services to an organization
  or give noncash gifts such as food, furniture, and
  clothing. We should avoid giving useless or junk
  gifts that take time to deal with and don't provide
  any value.

  2. We also may give something with an appreciated
  value (an asset that is now worth more than we
  paid for it). Examples include stocks, bonds, jew-
  elry, real estate, or anything that grows in value.

- *Drawing the line when it comes to borrowing—*

  1. Some organizations encourage people to borrow
  to give. We do not believe this kind of presumption
  on the future is scriptural. There is no example in
  Scripture of God ever using a loan to manifest His
  will in the lives of His people.

- *Taking a balanced approach to sacrificial giving—*

  1. Sacrificing to give is a way to honor God, but, once

again, this should be the result of a heart attitude and not a desire to impress others.

2. All of us have been called to suffer for Christ. *"For to you it has been granted for Christ's sake, not only to believe in Him, but also to suffer for His sake"* (Philippians 1:29). In America, this suffering has not included martyrdom or the abject poverty of many believers, but it has required an understanding that the purpose of our abundance is to further the kingdom of God. Very few have the problem of sacrificing too much.

Who Deserves My Support?

During the past few years, a number of well-known ministers have come under fire because of deception and lavish lifestyles. Their followers gave millions to support "ministry" activities at home and abroad but found out later that their contributions had been buying huge homes, extravagant cars, and other luxuries for ministry leaders.

If we want to be the best stewards possible of the money God has entrusted to us, we should ask at least three fundamental questions before giving God's money to an organization.

1. *Who are the people asking for the funds?* If we are not personally familiar with exactly what an organization does, we should get a list of references that we can verify through other well-known groups.

We should also ask for a doctrinal statement to determine whether the ministry is communicating a message true to Scripture. Notice how people respond to the message. Are goals being accomplished and is the ministry bearing fruit?

2. *For what purpose will the funds be used?* Ask for a projected budget. In some instances we may want to specify exactly where our gift will be applied.

3. *How are funds raised and managed?* It is wise to ask if a fundraising group is involved and what percentage of the funds go to that group. If more than 25 percent of the resources are being used for fundraising, we should be suspicious. A good indication of financial management is the debt/income ratio and changes in overhead expenses from year to year.

We should definitely avoid giving to ministries that use high-pressure fundraising techniques or questionable gimmicks (examples include special delivery letters, telegrams, and "miracle" items).

Insist on a copy of the ministry's annual budget and an audited financial statement for the previous year if you don't know the group well. Request a form called a "990" that nonprofit organizations file each year with the Internal Revenue Service.

Do not give to ministries whose leaders have rich and lavish lifestyles. The laborer is worthy of his hire, but a true servant of Christ will have a servant's attitude when it comes to material possessions. The ministry should maintain a high standard of excellence, along with freedom from waste.

The Evangelical Council for Financial Accountability (ECFA) investigates and reports financial responsibility in ministries:

ECFA (Evangelical Council for Financial Accountability)
440 West Jubal Early Drive
Suite 130
Winchester, VA 22601
1-800-323-9473

We don't offer these cautions to imply that most ministries are deceptive—any more than we would suggest that most $20 bills are counterfeit. But since the exceptions exist, we want to be able to recognize them. When you pray for God's wisdom, you can trust Him to guide your decisions.

Misused Gifts

We should be familiar with the organizations we support, but what if we give to an organization and later discover that it misuses God's money? Does that lessen the importance of our gift?

The answer is no. We have a responsibility to manage our giving as prudently as we manage our spending, but every penny we give "as unto the Lord" is still given to Him.

Although the Temple was greatly misused in Christ's time, He commended the widow for her two mites. Once again, God is concerned about our hearts.

Giving to Secular Causes

Non-Christian causes must be evaluated on an individual basis. There are many secular organizations that make good use of funds and perform much-needed community services.

For instance, if we enjoy watching the public television station in our area, we should support it. By becoming a regular contributor we will acquire more influence regarding the type of programs that are aired.

Many of us are asked to give to the United Way. There is nothing wrong in doing this as long as we reserve the right to select the organizations that will be helped by our donation. We are usually given a card to fill out that contains a long list of nonprofit groups from which we can choose.

Remember, all of this discussion regarding secular causes applies to giving beyond the tithe.

Section 3: Business Tithing

Tithing on the Increase

The principle of tithing from a business is not dramatically different from tithing personal income. Actually, most of the Scriptures on giving in the Old Testament deal with business-generated income, since few people were actually employees in the sense they are today.

The vast majority of people in Old Testament times were employed in agriculture, as were most Americans prior to the 1950s. The precedent for tithing from a business is clear in God's Word. Proverbs 3:9 says, *"Honor the Lord from your wealth and from the first of all your produce."*

Notice that the reference here is to farming. However, figuring a business tithe is not necessarily as clear-cut as figuring the tithe on one's personal income. For example, you should tithe on the business's increase, which is not usually the same as gross income.

Dealing with Noncash Assets

Business profits are often tied up in buildings, equipment, and vehicles, so it takes some creative thinking (and prayer) to decide how best to *"honor the Lord"* through your business.

A good example of this can be seen in farming. A farmer may say, "I hardly made anything this year," when, in fact, he added a combine, a new tractor, and another barn. The return was there, but it was in noncash assets. So how might we give in such a situation?

The answer for many Christians is to give a partial ownership in the business. That way, as the business prospers, so does God's portion.

Stanley Tamm is a good example of this. He developed a successful company called U.S. Plastics and deeded a portion of his company stock to a foundation established to do God's work. If a dividend was declared, the foundation got its share. If the company is ever sold, the foundation will get its equitable portion.

In the case of real property, such as buildings, trucks, and so on, tithing may be as simple as assigning God's portion of the property to our church or other ministry. Through the use of nonvoting stock, a company owner can do this without diluting his or her authority or decision-making ability.

Benefits of Stock Gifts

The gift of stock in a company can be

a double benefit to both the ministry and the businessperson. Since existing tax laws allow the value of a noncash gift to be claimed at its fair market value, the donor can receive a tax deduction at far above his or her actual cost. For instance, if a company's stock has a current market value of $100 per share, the donor receives a tax deduction of $100 per share even though his or her cost basis may only be $50 or $10 or even a few cents.

Since the stock wasn't actually sold by the donor, there is no capital gains tax due, so the entire gift value is a deduction. If the stock had been sold and the proceeds donated, the donor would have had to include the sale in total income for tax purposes and then deduct the gift.

Donating the stock prior to sale, therefore, represents a significant savings. If the ministry is a nonprofit organization, the stock can then be sold by them without incurring the capital gains tax.

Product Gifts

Many Christian business owners also have found that donating some of their products is an excellent way to support God's work. When we were refurbishing our ministry offices, a Christian who owned a window-blind company donated the blinds for all of our windows.

Other Christians have donated trucks, airplanes, food, and office equipment to ministries. But regardless of a gift's makeup, donors should be careful to give only what belongs to them, not what rightfully belongs to creditors, stockholders, or others.

Summary

Giving Is for Everyone

For the majority of Christians, serving God will never lead to worldwide fame, writing best-selling books, or singing before thousands of people. But regardless of the work to which we're called, there's hardly a follower of Christ who can't give; and when that giving is done in love, it exemplifies the greatest sacrifice ever made for mankind: the death of Jesus on the cross.

Jesus gave out of love when He laid aside His privileges and left heaven to come to earth. It was because of love that He became a servant and gave His life to save us from our sins. And the Bible tells us that God also was motivated by love when He gave His only begotten Son.

Along this line, Dr. Charles Ryrie made a powerful statement about love and money that lays bare the truth of our devotion.

"How we use our money demonstrates the reality of our love for God," he said. "In some ways it proves our love more conclusively than depth of knowledge, length of prayers, or prominence of service. These things can be feigned, but the use of our possessions shows us up for what we actually are."

To learn more about giving and tithing, check out the additional resources available from Crown.

- For Businesspeople: *Business by the Book* Independent Study by Larry Burkett, Howard Dayton, and David Rae (personal DVD video series) – ISBN# 1-56427-166-8

- For Children: *The ABC Learning Bank* from Crown Financial Ministries – ISBN# 1-56427-172-2

- For Anyone: *The Treasure Principle Workshop* video series by Randy Alcorn and Howard Dayton – ISBN# 1-56427-160-9

- For Anyone: *Your Money Map by Howard Dayton* – ISBN# 978-0-8024-6869-7

To purchase, contact your local Christian retailer or visit Crown online at Crown.org.

Mike And Liz Simpson's Story

More than 20 years ago, Mike and Liz Simpson were introduced to biblical financial principles through a Bible study written by Larry Burkett. After completing the material, they followed up by creating a spending plan using Larry's *Family Financial Workbook*.

"It changed our whole thinking," Mike says, "especially as far as tithing was concerned." One key lesson the couple learned was tithing from their firstfruits (Proverbs 3:9).

At the time, they were living in California. Their church didn't put a lot of emphasis on biblical financial teaching, and their pastor mentioned money from the pulpit only about once a year.

Mike didn't want to become caught up in legalistic thinking about money because he was "under grace." He laughs about it now, noting it was just an excuse to avoid tithing.

The study also prompted the couple to deal with another key issue: debt. "We had some small debts like credit cards, and another small loan, that we cleared up quickly," Mike says. "Then, we started working on our house. Within three and one-half years we were totally debt free and have been ever since."

A Personal Ministry

After their lives were changed by the Bible study and financial workbook, the Simpsons began sharing these materials with others through Bible studies in their home and church. They didn't push anything, and the first opportunities came sporadically. But as people's lives changed and they told others, the word began to spread. Mike says the future looks packed. "There are a lot of hurting people out there, and we're thrilled to see what the Lord is doing."

Changed Lives

Among the people Mike and Liz have taught throughout the years is a single mom whose husband left her with six children. She was depressed and "had no place to look but up," Mike says.

In addition, she was having a hard time accepting help. But the lessons she learned in the study not only hit home with her but with her entire family.

This impact played out in a life-changing word to the mother from one of her children—a daughter. Frustrated by financial and emotional pressure, the mother told her family that they didn't need charity.

In response, the daughter said, "Mom, remember what charity means? Love." These words had a powerful effect on this single mom, who was able to accept the help that local believers were trying to give her.

They should also have a powerful effect on us so that we never separate our giving from the motivation of love.

Freedom to Serve

For Liz and Mike themselves, the benefits of following God's financial principles include being able to give when God places opportunities in their path. The beneficiaries of this giving have included ministries, a church that needed help with a building program, and a single mom, to whom they provided food and financial help for more than a year. ■

Your Response

So what do I do now?

We encourage you to write at least one Action Step in response to the chapter you have just read. If you write more than one, prioritize them in a logical order so you have a clear first step that you can begin immediately.

Action Steps

_____

_____

_____

_____

_____

We also encourage you to reward yourself for every Action Step completed. Since the enemy ("the accuser") will do everything possible to discourage you by making the journey seem impossibly long, you need to see each step as its own victory. Your progress will be faster and more enjoyable if you take a little time to celebrate it.

Your celebration doesn't have to take a lot of time or money to be meaningful. Just make it something you enjoy, and tie it to the Action Step you have completed.

Celebration Plan

_____

_____

_____

_____

_____

_____

2 FIVE GROUPS OF GIVING CHRISTIANS

"Give, and it will be given to you. They will pour into your lap a good measure—pressed down, shaken together, and running over. For by your standard of measure it will be measured to you in return" (Luke 6:38). Few Scripture verses are quoted more often than Luke 6:38 regarding giving and receiving. But does it really mean what it seems to say? Does God promise to give to us abundantly? Do God's promises depend on our giving first? What about those who have nothing to give? Does that mean that they will receive nothing from the Lord?

The promise by Jesus recorded in Luke 6:38 was not made exclusively to the rich, spiritual, gifted, or talented. It was a promise to anyone who would apply its principles. Although the promise does include prerequisites, they are not prerequisites that involve one's spiritual maturity or social status. The prerequisites are ones of action: give first, then you will receive.

Giving types

Generally Christians are divided into five giving types or giving groups.[1]

- The first group either gives nothing or very little (far less than 10 percent of their incomes) to work being done in the Lord's name. It's ironic that most Christians in wealthier nations belong to this group.

- The second group gives at least 10 percent of their incomes regularly but seldom experiences what can be considered God's abundant material supply or spiritual bounty.

- The third group gives at least 10 percent of their incomes and can identify times when God has given to them both material and spiritual abundance.

- The fourth group is small. This group gives far above 10 percent of their incomes but seldom identifies with God's abundant material return.

- The fifth group is even smaller. This group gives far above 10 percent of the incomes and identifies with God's material and spiritual abundant return.

Those who give nothing or less than 10 percent of their income have, by their lack of giving, limited what God can do for them according to His Word. *"Will a man rob God? Yet you are robbing Me! But you say, 'How have we robbed You?' In tithes and offerings"* (Malachi 3:8). Paul the Apostle amplifies the same admonition. *"Now I say, he who sows sparingly will also reap sparingly, and he who sows bountifully will also reap bountifully"* (2 Corinthians 9:6). The lack of giving is an external indicator that there is something wrong spiritually.

Those who give more than 10 percent but not necessarily sacrificially and experience God's abundant supply are meeting God's prerequisites for where they are in their spiritual growth at that time. As they continue to grow and as God continues to teach them, the outward material abundance may change, as different lessons need to be learned.

Some of those who give far beyond 10 percent of their income and do not experience God's abundance could be giving with the wrong motive. They may be trying to bribe God; they require and even demand God's blessings because they gave, as they say, sacrificially. They are not in subjection to God but are trying to exercise control over Him.

But others in this category, who give abundantly but receive little physical evidence of God's return, may receive that return in other ways. These could include excellent health, a good and stable job, children and family who are committed to Christ, a car that seldom needs repairs, and so on.

The group who gives abundantly and receives abundance in return from the Lord, generally give because they desire to give, and although they may expect back from the Lord they do not demand it or become discouraged if they do not receive it in the manner or bounty they expected. Their giving is out of a desire to please God, not to profit from their relationship with Him. They are thankful when God gives back to them and show their thanks by giving back to God even more than they had given before the blessing.

Yet, they are also thankful even if God gives them nothing materially in return and will continue to give abundantly. Many in this group go through periods of overflowing abundance from the Lord, as well as long periods of no abundant return. But in either period, they continue to give because their desire is to give to the Lord's work. If they receive an abundant return from the Lord, they feel that the return was given so that they can give more.

If they do not receive an abundant return, they know that they are in the midst of a time of training and learning from the Lord for the next life's stage that He has prepared for them. As such, they usually conclude that their giving must not decrease but, rather, it should increase.

Conclusion

The spiritual principles behind Luke 6:38 are indeed giving and receiving, but we do not give to receive. The prerequisites to receiving are found in Luke 6:27-37. A Christian who lives by these principles practices the surrendered life. Therefore, the giving is simply a material expression of the deeper spiritual obedience to Christ.

Nearly every Christian desires to be obedient to God, and in many ways most are. However, Christ warned us that one of the greatest threats to our walk with God is the appeal of the materialist world. *"The one on whom seed was sown among the thorns, this is the man who hears the word, and the worry of the world and the deceitfulness of wealth choke the*

word, and it becomes unfruitful" (Matthew 13:22).

ENDNOTE

1. Adapted from *"Give and It Will Be Given to You"* by Larry Burkett.

Your Response

Action Steps _____

_____

_____

_____

_____

_____

_____

_____

_____

_____

_____

Celebration Plan _____

_____

_____

_____

_____

_____

_____

CHAPTER 3

CREATING A LIFESTYLE MINISTRY OF GENEROSITY AND BENEVOLENCE

Whether you are someone who

- wants to create a lifestyle of generosity and benevolence to others, and do it with God's wisdom,

- desires to grow spiritually and learn some practical ways to help others,

- desires to start an independent or church-sponsored benevolence ministry in your community, or

- wants a resource to share with your church as they consider how to start a benevolence ministry,

this chapter is invaluable in providing practical help and biblical insight for supporting others in a way that is fair, compassionate, and balanced.

Section 1: The Purpose of Welfare

First, let's broadly define a comprehensive benevolence ministry. It

- coaches individuals and couples with financial needs,

- provides them with work projects and income and,
- provides them with goods and services if needed.

Sherri, a young mother of two, struggled each month to meet her family's basic needs. Although she lived in a small apartment and owned a seven-year-old car, her income as a data entry employee was less than adequate. Her ex-husband was a chronic gambler who had divorced Sherri for another woman, moved out of state, and left her with $6,000 in credit card bills. Because her name was also on the credit card accounts, she was responsible for the charges.

To make matters worse, her car was in need of brakes, tires, a tune-up, and other service, but even a minor repair of $100 would strip her of any surplus funds for two to three months. Her appliances were simply left broken because she lacked the money to have them repaired.

One of the few bright spots in Sherri's life was her faith. She was a Christian and attended a major denominational church, but when she appealed to the benevolence committee for help, they sent her to the state welfare department.

She desperately wanted fellowship for herself and her children but no longer "fit" into a family unit. She also felt like an outcast who had been betrayed by a church to which she had tithed regularly for several years.

Imagine the disappointment in her faith when Sherri was told that the government, rather than God's people, could meet her needs.

The church's response is indicative of the way most Americans seem to view welfare—as a function of the government. But it is the church and its people, not the government, that He has made responsible for the administration of welfare.

Former President Ronald Reagan confirmed this fact when he proposed that every church and synagogue in the U.S. adopt 10 families beneath the poverty level. The result, he said, would be the elimination of all government welfare in this country.

A similar proposal was made by former New York Mayor Ed Koch, who asked the 350 churches and synagogues of his city to shelter 10 homeless people each night. Sadly, Koch received only seven positive replies. To make matters even worse, his proposal was actually criticized by priests, ministers, and rabbis.

But this problem is not confined to New York. The number of churches in America with effective benevolence ministries is so small that it is almost inconsequential.

Still, it is impossible to read the epistles of James and 1 John without recognizing the requirement to help others in need. John uses the lack of concern for the needs of others as evidence of a lack of love. *"But whoever has the world's goods, and sees his brother in need and closes his heart against him, how does the love of God abide in him? Little children, let us not love with word or wit tongue, but in deed and truth"* (1 John 3:17-18).

Therefore, we know that the true purpose of welfare (meeting the needs of others) is to be benevolent (to show kindness) so that God's love is demonstrated through us.

But the benefits of demonstrating God's love go much further than meeting physical needs. In 2 Corinthians 9:13 Paul wrote, *"Because of the proof given by this ministry, they will glorify God."*

Although the function of welfare is feeding people and caring for their needs, the purpose of welfare is drawing people to God by the physical expression of Christian love.

Obviously, the government's goal in welfare isn't drawing people to God. Therefore, the Bible has never made reference to the government as the administrator or distributor of welfare. It is a function of the body of Christ. The sooner we realize this and are willing to do something about it, the sooner others will come to God.

There is a great deal of talk about, and desire for, a revival in America today. We should remember that many revivals start as a result of the body of Christ acting as His literal hands, feet, and heart in a way that others are drawn to it.

SECTION 2: Who Qualifies for Help

Depending on the location of a particular church or organization, its benevolence ministry may receive a large number of help requests from strangers. Because these people are unknown, they may be tempted to turn them away. But Hebrews 13:2 tells us, *"Do not neglect to show hospitality to strangers, for by this some have entertained angels without knowing it."* As you consider whether to start a benevolence ministry or support an existing one with your time, talents, and treasures, never forget how joyful God is that you are willing to help and encourage others!

Transients

For benevolence ministries located near busy interstate highways, the majority of strangers may be transients (people who are passing through town on their way from one place to another). Such ministries must establish firm but fair rules for helping these people.

The number one rule is, do not give them cash. Common items needed by transients include food, lodging, and bus tickets. You can keep food stored at the ministry or make arrangements with a local restaurant to provide hot meals.

Lodging can be provided through arrangements with a local motel or hotel. And if a bus ticket is given, be sure the ticket helps the person reach a location where more help can be found.

The second rule is, check their references. Call people who know them and find out if their stories are true. Also find out if they do nothing but go from one benevolence ministry or church to another.

Some transients will use tragic stories that make them appear to qualify for help, and they may use the same stories at more than one ministry in a single town.

One way to identify them is to begin an inter-ministry referral system so that you and other individuals or ministries know who shows up at your door.

An example of this system is found in Dalton, Georgia, where Fellowship Bible Church has joined with other local churches and ministries to create a network that helps prevent fraud. Fellowship Bible Church keeps an extensive file of people who receive aid. Other ministries in the area also keep track of aid recipients.

A similar system for preventing fraud is a clearinghouse ministry, which involves the use of a central clearinghouse for help requests.

Widows, Single Parents, Orphans

Another group that qualifies for help and often needs long term assistance consists of widows, single parents, and orphans. Belmont Church in Nashville, Tennessee, has a special ministry for the benefit of these people.

The basis for this ministry is James 1:27, which says, *"Pure and undefiled religion in the sight of our God and Father is this: to visit orphans and widows in their distress, and to keep oneself unstained by the world."*

"We believe that 'widows and orphans' in modern-day America encompass single parents, the majority of whom are women," says Jim Davis, administrator of Belmont's benevolence ministry.

Single mothers may spend as much as half of their income on childcare. After housing, food, clothing, and medical costs are taken out, there isn't much left for emergencies.

"For these people, a simple car repair of $100 can become a major crisis in their finances," said Davis. "Such women and their children are under God special care. Psalm 68:5 (NIV) says the Lord is 'a father to the fatherless, a defender of widows.' The

Bible also tells us that while Jesus was on the cross, the two things He was concerned about were the salvation of a sinner and the care of His widowed mother."

Car repairs are just one of the problems faced by single parents and widows. To make matters worse, many do not know enough about cars to do routine maintenance or to recognize the early warning signs of problems. Therefore, they allow the problem to continue until their car breaks down, which usually results in huge repair bills that devastate their finances.

To help with these ongoing needs, Belmont has a Car Care Saturday once per quarter. On this day, members of the Men's Ministry and other volunteers change oil and do safety checks at no charge. Items such as belts, hoses, and brakes are inspected.

"The event is held in a warehouse owned by the church. Since the beginning of the ministry, a mechanic from the community has volunteered to oversee the work," Davis says. "We set up appointments for the women, and the volunteers gather at the garage around 9:00 A.M.

"Car Care Saturday has mobilized a lot of our men and provided a great place for male camaraderie and bonding. It also gives the men a wonderful outlet for service that they didn't have before."

Best of all, the ministry has become a magnet to attract people from outside the church. Remember, the function of welfare is to feed people and care for their needs, but the purpose of welfare is to draw people to God by the physical expression of Christian love.

If you have a special talent or skill that can be used to help someone—whether individually or as part of a benevolence ministry, look for an opportunity to be a blessing to others. Don't allow fear or uncertainty to keep you from helping someone. The Holy Spirit will guide you and give wisdom along with opportunities to serve.

If you personally know a single parent and would like to provide a resource to help them, we recommend *Financial Relief for Single Parents* by Brenda Armstrong (ISBN# 978-0-8024-4409-7). To order, contact your local Christian retailer or Crown for more information. Brenda also leads a ministry to help single parents and those who want to minister to them. For more information on additional resources for starting a ministry for single parents, contact Mercy Tree Ministries at MercyTree.org.

Prisoners and Their Families

Another group that deserves our help consists of prisoners and their families. People in prison have spiritual needs. Their families may also have spiritual needs, but they are almost certain to have physical needs.

Chuck Colson's Prison Fellowship Ministries represents an opportunity for churches to get involved in this much needed area of ministry. Prison Fellowship has led many prisoners to the Lord and provided economic assistance to their families. Part of this assistance is the annual Angel Tree project, which provides Christmas gifts to prisoners' children.

Needy People in Foreign Lands

Of course, the broad range of people qualifying for help is not limited to America. One part of your ministry as a believer in Christ or as part of a church body should be an outreach to starving people in other countries.

If your church doesn't participate in meeting this need, then support a good, independent ministry that feeds the hungry.

Fellow Church Members

James 2:15-16 stresses the importance of helping a fellow Christian in need. *"If a brother or sister is without clothing and in need of daily food, and one of you says to them, 'Go in peace, be warmed and be filled,' and yet you do not give them what is necessary for their body, what use is that?"*

And Galatians 6:10 says, *"While we have opportunity, let us do good to all people, and especially to those who are of the household of the faith."*

All benevolence work at Belmont Church is divided into two categories. One category involves people outside the church. The other involves the congregation and is referred to as "body ministry," because it is aimed at the church body.

"We believe we have a special obligation to minister to people who are part of our church body," says Belmont's Jim Davis. "That doesn't exclude other people, but we believe that we should be especially aware of our members' needs and be dedicated to addressing them."

Every member of any church should be able to look to the fellowship they attend as an extension of God's provision. They should feel the freedom to stand up and share their financial needs as freely as they would physical or spiritual needs. But, unfortunately, that's not always the case.

Pam had been a Christian nearly three years when her husband Cal decided he'd had enough of "religion" and told her he wanted a divorce. Cal was especially upset by Pam's Bible reading and her refusal to go drinking with him and his friends.

During the next several months he criticized her and eventually packed up and left. He provided Pam with about $500 a month, which was inadequate to support her and their three children.

After searching for a job that would at least meet her minimum needs, she ended up as a clerk for an insurance company, making about $1,000 a month. With two children in school, only her three-year-old son needed daycare, but the average fee of any decent daycare center pushed her spending plan to the limit.

In the meantime, Cal filed for divorce, which was granted on the grounds of incompatibility. The judge assigned child support of $375 a month, and suddenly Pam found herself in a financial deficit as the expenses exceeded her income. She made the seemingly necessary cuts in her budget, including car maintenance and clothing. Then, her pastor called and asked if she would come by his office at the end of the week.

She spent the next several days wondering what he might want. Perhaps he wants to know if we have any needs, she thought. Hers was a caring church that ministered to some of the poor in their community.

But when she arrived at the pastor's office, he informed her that her membership had been suspended because of the divorce. "But I didn't divorce my husband," Pam protested. "He divorced me. I wouldn't even agree to the divorce. But in this state either spouse can get a divorce if the judge agrees."

Despite Pam's argument, church leaders refused to change their minds. In the process of judging her actions, they had completely overlooked her needs. They also lost a member who could have made important contributions to their church.

Pam joined another church, where she was warmly received and played a role in the establishment of a daycare ministry. With the aid of an anonymous $50,000 donation, the ministry expanded over the next two years to care for nearly 60 children, including a summer ministry for latchkey kids.

If Christians are denied assistance or are shunned by a church, they often learn to keep their needs to themselves and develop an attitude of isolation, believing that nobody— including God, the local church, or other Christians—cares about their needs. Many of them leave the church and begin looking for aid from other sources. If they have not developed a trust in God or other Christians, they often will turn to the government for help when what they really need is relationship, guidance, and training.

Acts of benevolence and personal involvement through small groups and financial coaching are discipleship tools that show God's love in tangible ways.

SECTION 3: Getting Started

Before practicing welfare, ministries first should be careful to meet a number of prerequisites, including the establishment of a Benevolence Committee. There should be three separate spiritual gifts represented among the membership of the committee: the gift of helps, the gift of mercy, and the gift of administration.

In addition, it helps to have a broad range of people serving in benevolence, including people of different ages, genders, and marital status. This diversity provides a balanced approach to administering benevolent funds and services.

Keeping appropriate boundaries in relationships with those in need is difficult. The book, *Boundaries* (Zondervan), by Dr. Henry Cloud and Dr. John Townsend, provides insight on how to maintain perspective about your responsibilities.

Some people who need benevolent assistance may have needs for professional services they cannot acquire because of their financial situation. It helps to locate doctors, lawyers, electricians, plumbers, etc., who would be willing to donate services from time to time for a needy person. It is important to make limited referrals to these professionals rather than to broadcast their services. This will protect them from being overextended and will ensure their willingness to serve.

Developing Guidelines

One of the Benevolence Committee's first jobs will be to develop guidelines for itself, including what kind of assistance will be provided, how much assistance will be provided, and how people will apply for assistance.

Furthermore, it is very important that guidelines be established for coordinating the work of any smaller committees under the authority of the Benevolence Committee.

For example, a benevolence ministry may have a Body Ministry Committee, a Widows and Orphans Committee, an Unemployed People's Committee, or an Overseas Ministry Committee.

Financial coaching is another area that needs to be dealt with. A church or organization's financial ministry may be separate from its benevolence ministry, but it is important that both ministries within the same church or organization work together.

One other job for the Benevolence Committee is to determine if it will recommend government assistance programs for people who qualify for help from such programs.

SECTION 4: Standards for Helping

Everyone from outside a particular church or ministry who is seeking help should be required to go through a screening process. This screening may begin with completion of a questionnaire like the sample that appears at the end of this book. For needs within the congregation, individuals and families should be interviewed, but most of the needed information should be assessed through financial coaching. Any candidates for ongoing help should be required to participate in a financial study like Crown's Life Group.

Money Map Coaching

Along with screening, people seeking help should be required to submit to financial coaching—either one-time or ongoing, according to the assistance they need.

Couples should be coached together. Single people should not be coached by someone of the opposite gender if it can be avoided. When it cannot be avoided, there should always be a third party on the premises with a clear view of the meeting area. Failure to do this will place both people in a potentially compromising position.

The Proper Setting for Coaching

It is important that the setting for coaching be as neutral as possible. Therefore, meeting in the coach's home is not recommended. A home setting often results in disruptions that impair good communication. In addition, coaches need to protect their family time. People with great needs can sometimes take advantage of a coach's concern, so contact should be limited to scheduled appointments.

The church or other supportive ministry environment is a good neutral place conducive to coaching. People who feel uncomfortable in a church setting may not be receptive to advice based on God's Word.

Coaching Transients

If applicants are transients, there probably won't be an opportunity for long-term, in-depth financial coaching. This type of coaching is best suited for people the

church or organization is helping on a longer-term basis. However, this doesn't prevent sharing some basic financial principles with transients.

Of course, the main coaching effort with transients should be spiritual, with a focus on sharing the gospel.

SECTION 5: The Need for Teaching and Coaching

Why is this so important? Crown Life Groups provide accountability and support as its members learn biblical principles. Coaches can detect spiritual and financial problems in the life of a person seeking help.

Spiritual Problems

A common spiritual problem is materialism, which causes people to spend beyond their means or spend too much on luxuries. As a result, they may suddenly find they don't have enough to cover the cost of necessities. This so-called crisis is only the external symptom of an internal problem.

Be encouraged that God can change any heart and fix any emotional or financial challenge people face. He simply uses coaches and other volunteers to facilitate what He wants to accomplish.

Financial Problems

Lack of money for necessities may also result from financial problems such as poor money management (lack of a spending plan).

Guidance Problems

Some families that struggle to manage their money may never have been taught how. Some, like single parents, suffer sudden drops in income or have needs that exceed their income.

More than a "Band-Aid"

It is not wrong to help people in situations like these, even though they may be at fault. However, the person must be willing to follow the recommendations of the coach in order to receive help.

Too often a local benevolence ministry amounts to the pastor directing the secretary to write someone a check for food, gas, or rent. That is usually the worst thing a ministry could do.

Without accountability, giving more money can be like pouring gasoline on a fire.

At Fellowship Bible Church, whose inter-organizational referral system was discussed briefly in Section 2, no money is given through the benevolence ministry unless there's financial coaching involved.

The church's goal, according to Pastor Jim Burgess, is to avoid putting "Band-Aids" on people's problems.

"The first thing we do in benevolence is to focus on salvation, which is the spiritual area," Burgess says. "Then, we try to focus on the financial area."

Establish a Spending Plan

People (other than transients) receiving help from a benevolence ministry should be willing to draft a spending plan with the aid of a Money Map coach and also a mentor, if needed. This plan should include a commitment to no more debt.

Teaching and *Money Map* coaching are important because the average family seeking help usually has enough money; they just don't know how to manage it. However, as the ministry takes on more of the role of welfare, it will encounter more coaching participants, especially single parents, who do not make enough money to provide for basic needs. A spending plan enables the ministry to discover specific deficits that need to be met and helps them provide accountability. Crown Financial Ministries has developed resources to prepare any church or organization to deal with specific single-parent needs.

Two cautions that every *Money Map* coach should be aware of:

1. Do not make recommendations in a judgmental way.
2. Do not make recommendations that you would not be willing to follow.

Other Financial Ministry Functions

Outside of coaching in benevolence cases, church-based financial ministries can provide other important services, such as training the rest of the congregation in biblical money management.

Financial Studies

Everyone in the congregation should be encouraged to participate in a Life Group study on the biblical principles of money management. Crown's study frees the congregation financially to support the work of the church and its benevolence. In particular, every person from the congregation who comes to the Benevolence Committee for help should be required to attend a Life Group study. Even though their funds are low, these people will begin to learn how to put God in control of their finances and make wise decisions. It may be necessary to have mentors, who have already gone through the study, available to assist those who are receiving benevolent help, especially if this is their first experience with handling money.

Crown seminars prepare churches for the Life Group studies, coaching, and receiving single parents.

"Journey to True Financial Freedom Se∆62

minars" covers biblical stewardship principles, debt management, and basic spending plan techniques in a six-hour format.

"Business by the Book Seminars" present biblical principles for operating your business through lectures, case study discussions, and sharing experiences.

"Crown Money Map Coach Training Workshops" equip individuals to do budget counseling in their church or local community.

"Crown Life Group Leader Training" events train leaders to lead all Crown Teaching Solution studies and materials.

"Single Parent Ministry Training" (SPMT) trains the churches in the right and wrong ways to help and how to set up

specific ministries to meet the practical needs of single parents: car care, housing, child care, etc. To learn more about SPMT training specifically, contact Mercy Tree Ministries at MercyTree.org.

Money Map Coaches

Volunteer Money Map coaches work through their local churches to provide coaching to people who write or call Crown Financial Ministries for help. Callers are referred to the nearest church, business, or organization equipped with trained leaders and resources from Crown, including more than 1,200 Money Map coaches throughout the United States.

For information about the Money Map Coach Training Course, seminars, or other Crown resources, visit us online at Crown. org, call 1-800-722-1976, or write to Crown Financial Ministries, PO Box 100, Gainesville, GA 30503.

SECTION 6: A Willing Attitude

In the previous section, we noted that people who receive help must be willing to follow their coach's recommendations. In addition, they must be willing to work, unless they are disabled or, in the case of some single parents, are unable to pay for child care on their income. In either case, a benevolence ministry along with the support of a local church can assist in overcoming the obstacles to self-sufficiency.

Many times, able-bodied people who are out of work aren't willing to work, especially those who receive some type of public assistance. Unless the ministry offers access to medical care or child care, many of these people will refuse to work because they believe they have too much to lose in benefits.

Other able-bodied people will want to pick jobs selectively that fit their education, personalities, and all the rest. Although we encourage these people to discover and use their gifts and talents, they need to be willing to work if a job is available, at least for a short time, even when it isn't a perfect fit.

The apostle Paul said in II Thesssalonians 3:10, *"If anyone is not willing to work, then he is not to eat, either."* In previous centuries, the church gave assistance only to individuals who passed a "work test." Men and women worked for their food by chopping wood or sewing clothes for other needy families. The same thing can be accomplished today by directing needy people to jobs or giving them work to do around the ministry or church.

Unless they show a willingness to shoulder some of the responsibility and work, generally they are not willing to help themselves. As you're showing the love of Christ and being an encouragement to needy people, remember to stay balanced and make sure they do their part in the process. Doing all of the work for them will do more harm than good on a long-term basis.

Willingness and Spiritual Training

Willingness, or a lack thereof, also shows in a person's attitude about spiritual training. Everyone being coached financially should be required to learn the biblical aspects of managing finances because it is God's Word that provides lasting transformation. Crown offers a variety of ways to offer this service. Two of our popular studies are:

- *How to Manage Your Money* work book and *Family Financial work book* (for individual study)

- The 10-week Biblical Financial Study Life Group study (for small groups)

Coaching participants should be required to complete a portion of their Bible study between each coaching session. If they haven't done their homework, the next session should be canceled. We don't want to be guilty of dealing with the symptom, which is usually financial, and ignoring the problem, which usually has spiritual components—especially if we include ignorance and immaturity under the spiritual umbrella.

God's Word: The Only Real Remedy

When it comes to spiritual problems, no amount of money or any other kind of help can substitute for the solution found in God's Word. Lost people need salvation, and saved people need to live according to God's will.

Unfortunately, our society fails to recognize this fact and responds with its own solutions. But only God can fill the void in people's lives.

If money could satisfy every need, society wouldn't be looking elsewhere for answers. One example is the spread of the New Age Movement among wealthy celebrities, which is unfortunate, because this path will only lead them to more frustration and a bigger letdown.

Syndicated columnist George Will said that our crumbling fiscal and social society needs another John Wesley, who rode Britain's rural roads and city streets, evangelizing the underclass, exhorting pride, and combating family disintegration by teaching people to change their behavior.

Wesley's efforts had a tremendous effect on Britain, because the solution he brought to the masses was the right one. You can't simply hand out money and expect that people's basic nature will change. Jesus Christ is the positive life changer.

SECTION 7: Needy or Greedy?

Some time ago, a reporter disguised himself as a homeless person and spent a month with homeless people in New York City. Following this experience, he reported that the homeless people he'd traveled around with were content to eat off the system but absolutely were not interested in fundamental lifestyle changes.

Some had actually come from well-to-do families and had "escaped the system," to use their own words. They laughed about the free publicity they were receiving from the press as a result of the current "help the homeless" campaign. They had chosen their lifestyle and were not going to change.

Unfortunately, such people consume the funds intended to help people with genuine needs, like people who are homeless as the result of a financial catastrophe. Chances are these latter people will change if given the opportunity.

The same holds true for needy people in many other situations. At the same time, there are people who are content to rely

on the church on a long-term basis with no motivation to work or improve their situation. How do you distinguish between them and the person who really needs help?

Dealing with Fraud

Unfortunately, no system for dealing with fraud is fail-safe, but there are precautions that ministries and churches can take, such as the transient policy we discussed in Section 2. Longer-term help must be accompanied by willingness to follow a coach's recommendations and go to work if a job is made available. Screening questionnaires for applicants and establishing an inter-ministry network are important precautions.

Unfortunately, people who operate benevolence ministries must be investigators as well as helpers. And one of their key concerns should be the stories of the applicants.

Following up on stories has already been recommended in

the case of transients, but it applies to longer-term cases as well. This won't always be easy because some people will take offense. But it's necessary if a ministry wants to control fraud.

As an example, let's look again at the benevolence ministry of Fellowship Bible Church.

"Usually in every case, or at least partially, we'll do some kind of checking to see if the person's stories add up," says Fellowship pastor Jim Burgess. "We believe that as long as this is done in love, not in a judgmental manner, people who have genuine needs will respond positively. Many people walk away, but we do feel that those who stay genuinely need the help."

Considering the number of applications some ministries receive, checking up on stories may seem like a huge task, but people who are telling the truth will do what they can to help verify what they've told you.

Also consider whether their stories are believable. Are key facts missing? Have the applicants, in an effort to convince you, given a tremendous amount of detail that isn't relative to the main point of the stories?

Furthermore, consider whether the applicants have "forgotten" key information, given only partial answers to your questions, or tried to change the subject.

Finally, are the applicants demanding immediate action so you won't have time to consider their requests? Are they trying to make you feel guilty for doubting their honesty?

Applicants who employ tactics like these are more likely to be dishonest. In this case, the ministry will have to deny their requests until they are willing to make necessary changes and become productive members of society.

It's a difficult situation, but any time you operate a benevolence ministry, you take on the problems that go along with it; and some of those problems are frustrating. Despite that fact, it's still the responsibility of God's people to meet needs of those within the church and, to the degree possible, those outside the church.

SECTION 8:
Know Your Resources

Any individual, church, or organization that desires to start a benevolence ministry should be aware of the resources available within the congregation. This includes financial resources (money) and physical resources (people).

Many people have skills and abilities that can be useful to a benevolence ministry. Skilled laborers like plumbers, carpenters, roofers, electricians, appliance repairers, mechanics, and many other services and skills can match needs in the congregation. These people may be willing to fix a problem that is referred by benevolence at little or no cost. It is important that the referrals come through benevolence, because broadcasting their willingness to serve may cause them to be overwhelmed with needs, and they will quickly burn out. Limit referrals to the number of people they are willing to help over a given period of time.

The ministry can also use these volunteers by hosting regular "fix-it" days. This is usually done seasonally, once per quarter. People with needs sign up and indicate the items they need fixed, and the ministry recruits volunteers who are able to fix the problems. By sending workers in teams, the work is done quickly and there is no question about propriety for men working in the homes of single women.

These people who can use their work skills to meet needs aren't the only physical resources required to operate a benevolence ministry. Volunteers without specialized skills can screen applicants or deliver food to shut-ins. They simply need to care enough about the needs of others to be willing to inconvenience themselves in order to help.

Outside of skilled labor and volunteers, there are other resources that can be helpful to a benevolence ministry.

Job Sources

Locate sources of jobs for people who apply for help and are willing and able to work. One church met this challenge by establishing a job ministry. It was linked to the church building program so that when unemployed people came in they could help with the construction.

They actually hammered, sawed, and painted under the supervision of a trained layperson. Money had been donated by others within the local church, not only to employ people but to actually build the building.

However, this brings up questions about tax reporting and liability. Churches should consider the extent of their liability if a worker is hurt on the job and whether these workers should be designated as employees or independent contractors.

Of course, church building programs are not the only way to put people to work. The church we've just discussed also made an effort to find members who had businesses that required part-time help.

One of these businesses was a mailing service; another was a parking service. These jobs didn't pay much, but they reduced the amount of church money needed to help people get back on their feet.

When helping with job and career options, one popular resource that has served thousands of people is the *Career Di-*

rect® Complete Guidance System. More than a career assessment, *Career Direct®* analyzes four key areas—personality, skills, interests, and values—to maximize how people can use their God-given talents and skills in life and work. To learn more about *Career Direct®* and the ability to offer this assessment at a discounted rate as a part of your benevolence ministry, go to CareerDirectOnline.org.

Surplus Goods

Many churches and organizations have what they call an "Elijah's Barrel" or "God's Storehouse," to which members donate food, clothes, and toys for the specific purpose of distributing to needy families who have gone through financial training and coaching. This resource is also useful in providing help to transients.

If a ministry has space for a food pantry, it may "glean" many products such as bread, produce, canned goods, or meats from area stores and retail wholesalers who will donate the items if the ministry picks them up as scheduled. Other ministries and churches purchase bulk items, government surplus, or co-op foods to distribute.

Storing clothes takes space for storage and enough volunteers to sort the clothing for usability and size. Then someone needs to be available to distribute the clothing.

Solving the Clothing Dilemma

Most donated clothing is out-of-date or is too worn to use. It is often the clothing that someone couldn't sell at a garage sale or consignment shop. Ministries that receive clothes usually receive much more than they can distribute. That is why many don't take in clothing.

Unneeded clothing and other items the ministry may not have room to store can be donated to second-hand stores for vouchers for needy applicants to redeem. Other ministries offer clothing exchanges a few times a year. On specified days, individuals and families bring in their own clothing and choose clothing brought in by others. All the remaining clothing is either taken home by the people who brought it or sent to Goodwill or the Salvation Army.

One church has a unique way of handling clothing distribution by combining it with its annual Single Parent Expo, which is an all-day conference for single parents. The event and childcare are provided for a small fee and includes workshops on topics of interest.

Professional or work clothing is donated by businesswomen or area clothing retailers and hung on racks in a room near the ladies' restroom, which is used as a dressing room during the event. The women put on a fashion show during the lunch-time; then the women are invited by tables to try on and select two outfits to take home. All participants benefit.

Another organization stores donated professional clothing for job seekers. They give one outfit for a job interview and another one when a job is secured. This is a great way to provide incentives for those who do not have appropriate work clothing.

SECTION 9: Where Does It Begin?

A benevolence ministry originates with one person who says, "I believe God called me to do that." If that person is you, don't hesitate to begin a ministry in your church or community.

Remember, it's not enough simply to see a need; you must accept the challenge of meeting that need. Many individuals have seen the need and met the challenge.

Jenny Forner worked closely with an interchurch network in Grand Rapids, Michigan, for several years and witnessed firsthand the needs of low-income families. To meet the need Jenny developed New Focus, a ministry that assists needy families with financial coaching, community and church resource information, benevolence help, and mentoring through ongoing relationships.

In Coos Bay, Oregon, a remarried mother of two teens became concerned about the needs of single mothers in her church and community. She had heard about the car care ministry at Belmont Church on the radio and was encouraged. Coos Bay is a small community and not many resources are available. This mom called together several members of her church and asked them to pray about what they could do.

The small group of men and women decided to start a car care ministry. Once a month in the church parking lot, the men do oil changes and maintenance inspections for women who agree to attend a single-mom's meeting that is held at the same time as the car care.

During the meeting, the women eat a light breakfast, sing praise songs, hear a message for single moms, and receive prayer for their needs. The goal is to train moms in parenting and offer job possibilities. One person demonstrated cake decorating and offered an apprenticeship to any mom who wanted to learn more.

The church also offers a clothing exchange. Additional volunteers from the church care for the children during the meeting, taking them bowling or out for ice cream or some other fun activity.

What makes this ministry remarkable is that the church is not large, fewer than 100 families, and they want to do more.

Another ministry, Christians in Action in Minnesota, started with a couple who were Crown Money Map coaches. Through coaching low-income families, they began to notice a widespread problem. The rural setting required most people to have cars, but because of high housing expenses, many could not afford car maintenance, clothing, or other necessities—even if they were working.

The couple selected some other couples from other churches to join them in developing a plan of assistance. One of the men, a garage owner, offered car repairs at cost for the women being helped if the church would assist in the cost and would supply volunteers.

They had no problem finding volunteers and began offering oil changes and minor repairs once a month. During the car care, they teach the women biblical

principles for handling money. Money Map coaches are available to work with the women one-to-one if needed. The ministry also provides a hot meal and a clothing exchange. During the monthly event, the ministry distributes produce, bread, and other food to those in need in the community.

Although these efforts were very helpful, they didn't solve the problems of women whose cars needed larger repairs or replacement. When a local newspaper featured the ministry in a story, however, Christians and non-Christians alike donated so many cars that the garage owner had to get a dealer's license to distribute them. Some cars that were too large or too expensive to maintain were sold to individuals; cars that were not roadworthy were sold as junk, with the proceeds going into the ministry fund to provide needed repairs.

Someone from the area heard what they were doing and gave a sizeable donation. The garage owner obtained liability insurance just for the ministry and now offers cars and most repairs on the basis of what the Money Map coaches say the women can afford.

These ministries began because of the commitment of one person. Starting a benevolence ministry in your church or community will require a commitment of time and resources, but you can do it. And the resulting ministry can transform the lives of people who would not otherwise see the gospel in action.

Learn God's Financial Principles

Also, it is important that you, members of the Benevolence

Committee, and especially any who will do financial coaching, become trained in God's principles of handling money. The seminars discussed in Section 5 can help you move toward this goal. In addition, everyone in the ministry or church should be encouraged to participate in a Crown Life Group study on biblical financial principles. This study ultimately frees others financially to support the work of the church and benevolence.

All congregation members coming to the Benevolence Committee for help should be trained in biblical money management. Even though funds are low, they will learn to make wise decisions, and they will grow in their trust of God's provision. They may need mentors who already have gone through the study, especially if this is their first experience with deliberate money management.

As the organizer of the benevolence ministry, it is advisable for you to be trained as a Crown Money Map coach. Many others in your church or organization will probably need this training as well to coach all those who have needs.

Where will all these people come from? There are plenty of caring people; they just need someone to be a catalyst—to cast a vision and begin organizing them. Once these committees get started, they are usually overwhelmed with help.

And remember that if God has led you to start a benevolence ministry in your church or community, He will meet your needs in many creative and wonderful ways as you trust Him.

SECTION 10:

Community Benevolence

If you've ever seen a church or other organization with a comprehensive benevolence
ministry, you know the tremendous amount of
good that just one body of believers can do.

But imagine what could be accomplished if many individuals, churches and/or organizations in your town joined
together to assist people in need.

This joint effort, which might be called "community benevolence," has become popular and successful in communities
throughout the country.

In this section, we'll look at several community benevolence
ministries that could be started by you or someone else in
your church or community.

Community Clearinghouse

One of the most successful approaches to community benevolence is a model established in 1976, when its founder, Virgil
Gulker, worked for the Good Samaritan Center, a church-
supported helping agency in Holland, Michigan.

Like other helping agencies, the center was in constant need
of volunteers, but people in local churches offered little help.

After spending some time thinking about the situation, Gulker
came to a conclusion. His agency was an intermediary. On
one side were people with all sorts of needs (food, housing,
emotional counseling, financial coaching), and on the other
side were church members, who were not involved and ap-
peared not to care. Yet they had some money to offer.

"We took money from the church people and provided services to the needy," says Gulker in his book *Help Is Just Around the Corner.*[1] "We were in between on the churches' behalf. But now it struck me that we were also in between as a barrier.

"We were separating church members from those in need. Our organization shut off the church members from the very people their money was serving. And the better we did our job, the more effective a barrier we became.

"Our success made it less and less necessary for church members ever to have anything to do with needy people in person."

Gulker wondered if there wasn't an untapped reservoir of believers who wanted to minister personally to the needy but couldn't because of the barriers that helping agencies had erected.

He met with local agencies and pastors to discuss the situation, and what evolved from those meetings was a new concept in benevolence. It involved the use of a central clearinghouse to determine the nature, extent, and legitimacy of needs.

People who were seeking help would come to the clearinghouse first. After their needs were analyzed, they would be sent either to an agency or a church for help.

If they had a specialized need, the center would refer them to a specialized organization. But if the person needed some type of help not provided by an agency, the center would send them to a church.

The tremendous response was a welcome answer to Gulker's question about hidden resources. In a short time, 74 churches in Holland, representing 13 denominations, were involved.

Perhaps the reason so many people were volunteering for the center is that it provided ministry opportunities to a broad range of people. The volunteers came from many groups, including the young, the old, the wealthy, the poor, the highly educated, and the less educated.

Some of these people had never been asked to minister before; they gladly accepted the opportunity when it became available.

Each local church or organization that joins a center selects one or two members as contact persons to be trained by the center. One of their first responsibilities is to survey members of their church or organization to determine the areas in which they're willing to serve. For many church members, this provides their first opportunity for personal ministry involvement.

Ministry options on the survey include plumbing, painting, visiting the elderly, translating a language, helping people fill out forms, or simply being a caring friend to someone who is alone.

Doors to ministry that seemed shut for the average member are now open. In one church, 75 percent of the membership volunteered its services.

1. Used by permission of Creation House, Altamonte Springs, Florida, from *Help Is Just Around the Corner,* by Virgil Gulker, © 1988.

More than 1,800 Christians volunteered after a center was established in Fresno, California.

But volunteers aren't the only people who benefit from the center's approach. The ministry is designed to meet the root causes of needs and not simply to throw money at the problems of people seeking help.

One of the ministry's goals is to lead people to Christ. Doors for witnessing are opened through Bible-based materials, and for some people, this is their first exposure to the Scriptures.

In addition, this combination of meeting physical needs and witnessing is typical of Christ's ministry on earth.

This approach uses a four-step helping process that begins when someone calls a local clearinghouse. "The clearinghouse is principally a phone ministry," says Pat Johnson, an affiliate director. "It's like a 'ministry 911.' The exception is that we're not emergency care; we're lifestyle care."

Volunteers at the clearinghouse gather the information necessary to analyze the client's need. The actual analysis takes place in the second step of the ministry, when needs are also verified.

"Once the analysis has been done, we'll make a decision on the most appropriate referrals for this individual," Mrs. Johnson says.

The third step is actually referring the client to a church, agency, or organization. However, the client is responsible for making the contact.

"We'll tell clients what they must do, but we don't do it for them," Mrs. Johnson says. "Our contention is that they need

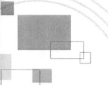

to take those self-help steps in order to become productive in their own lives. If we keep on doing those things for them, we're just creating chronic dependents.

"If we find people who are chronically dependent, or systems users, we won't turn them away, but we will require them to meet certain conditions. For example, in order to receive assistance next week, we might require that three employment applications be filed."

The fourth and final step of the center's ministry is follow-up. "We check back to see if the client was helped," Mrs. Johnson says. "Then, the client is offered a visit from a pastor or church member in [his or her] area."

In her early days with the center, when she served as a ministry director, Mrs. Johnson found that 70 percent of the people said "yes" to these pastoral visits.

As already noted, the concept is growing. But one obstacle faced by the ministry is the way it is perceived by pastors. They fear that if their church becomes involved in a center it will jam even more work into their already crowded schedules. But many pastors have found the reverse is actually true.

"The number one fear," Mrs. Johnson says, "is that churches believe this type of center is an inter-faith project, which will cause their doctrines to be watered down."

However, she adds, "We don't even touch their doctrines. We act as an extension ministry office for each church, and all we do is set their people up to minister. Then, they minister according to their own doctrines, teachings, and so forth."

Crown Financial Ministries works closely with these types of ministries to spread biblical alternatives to government welfare across America. This partnership between parachurch organizations is just a small illustration of the huge partnerships that have developed between churches and centers throughout the U.S. The following story from Gulker's book illustrates how effective these partnerships can be.

If it hadn't been for the women's glasses he was wearing, Rob would have looked almost normal. As it was, he seemed in better shape than the other men at the rescue mission. He didn't smell of alcohol, and from the look of his eyes it didn't appear that he was using drugs.

In the opinion of Alan Doswald, a center director in Fresno, California, Rob didn't appear to be very far from the path back into ordinary life. Alan had first met Rob during a visit to the rescue mission with several other Christians.

During a later visit to the mission, he offered to help Rob come in off the streets. When Rob accepted, Alan began to pray and make phone calls.

A needs analysis done by a center determined that there were no warrants out for Rob's arrest. And the life story he gave proved to be true. So Alan began seeking a place for Rob to stay.

A parishioner of a nearby church who made a living by buying, repairing, and reselling apartments was willing to have Rob stay in a place he was fixing up. But when he met Rob, he invited him to stay in his own home.

Rob's need for clothes was handled by two church-operated clothing closets. Another church donated bedding and towels. From another church came a man who worked with the department of rehabilitation. He sat down with Rob and helped him develop a résumé.

Rob contacted an old friend and got a job selling cars. Then he needed good clothes. Two churches chipped in $150 each so he could buy some.

To help him get to work, another church bought him a bus pass for a month. And a Christian optometrist made him a new pair of glasses.

To take care of him after that, someone donated a used car. It needed minor repairs and a new transmission.

A mechanic from one church made the repairs free of charge, and a mechanic from another church installed the new transmission.

While all of this was happening, a church was collecting furniture for the day when Rob would be able to move into his own place. Altogether, Christians belonging to eight churches in town helped Rob get his life together again.

Recently Alan asked Rob what it was that finally motivated him to come in off the streets. "I decided to give it a try because someone really cared about me," he answered. "That gave me hope."

If you're interested in establishing a community clearinghouse where you live, call 800-777-5277 for more information.

Community Funds

In one city, churches established a community benevolence fund that was administered by the local police department.

If a church determined that a needy person qualified for money from the fund, the church would call the police department in advance to let them know that the person would be arriving and how much he or she was to be given.

Such a ministry demands great cooperation between all parties involved, strict guidelines for operation, and a willingness on the part of all churches to contribute their fair share of money.

Community Care and Share

Several churches, ministries, and organizations can join together to establish a care-and-share center where people can get food, used clothing, used toys, and other needed items.

Again, all organizations involved must be willing to give their fair share.

Trust Funds

If someone in the community is facing tremendous medical expenses, ministries can join together to establish and support a trust fund for that person.

Crown Financial Ministries recommends that ministries consult a tax attorney about the establishment of such a fund.

SECTION 11: Welfare that Works

One would think that with all the billions spent on welfare since the 1960s, poverty would not exist. But that's not the case. The reason: Indiscriminate welfare traps its recipients by making them dependent.

To make matters worse, our federal welfare system consumes more than 80 percent of its allocation in administrative overhead.

In contrast, biblical welfare gives more than just money. It also meets the need for spiritual and financial training in people's lives. And it looks toward restoring them to positions of productivity.

Although millions of people have left welfare through welfare reform, they are now the working poor, with an average annual income below the poverty line. In addition, there are still millions on the system or entering it for the first time. Helping people get off welfare and become a part of the workforce is a major need in our society, and the body of Christ can play a role in meeting this need—one person at a time. It takes commitment from everyone involved, but it can be done and God will bless it in amazing ways.

In Gainesville, Georgia, where Crown Financial Ministries is located, a woman named Mary Brawner gladly tells how she got off welfare with the help of her church.

As you read this story, consider what your church or benevolent organization is doing to meet the needs of others. Then, determine what you can do to help or, if necessary, begin such a ministry.

 Mary Brawner lived in government subsidized housing. She was about to begin receiving Social Security benefits for her oldest son, which she planned to invest. She was already receiving some income from a part-time job at a local hospital and hoped this job would eventually lead to full-time employment.

But when officials in charge of the subsidized housing learned that Mary would be receiving the Social Security check, they raised her rent by an equal amount. Mary's church offered to help her if she would commit to work and see a Money Map coach. She agreed and was amazed at how much difference a spending plan made in her life.

When Mary was finally ready to break away from the welfare system, there was one last hurdle she had to clear. She lost a number of benefits, such as medical care and food stamps, which now she would have to pay for herself. It was at this critical point, which lasted about four weeks, that Mary needed help most from the church. Without that help, she might have been driven back onto welfare.

Today, she is receiving medical insurance through her job and supporting herself completely. She also has life insurance, which she didn't have before.

"If the church had just given me money without pushing me to get on a spending plan, I would still be on welfare," Mary says. "Living on welfare made me feel trapped, like I was in prison. My pastor always taught that believers in Christ and the church, not the government, should administer welfare. Now I see the truth of that message."

Suggestions for Food Ministries

There are many approaches to operating a food ministry. The most common method is to have an on-site storage room that

is open to those in need during scheduled hours. Food may be obtained as
donations from area markets, producers,
outlets, and distributors. You also may have
regular food drives in your church or community. The following is a list of the most commonly
stored items.

- Staples (dried beans, flour, corn meal, sugar, pasta, rice, shortening or oil, crackers)
- Canned fruit, vegetables, soups, fruit juice
- Cereals, oatmeal, grits, dry milk
- Canned meat or fish, peanut butter, jelly
- Convenient foods (macaroni and cheese, canned meals, pasta sauces)
- Baby needs (cereal, formula, juice, diapers)
- Transient items: individual pop-top cans of prepared food (beef stew, chicken/ dumplings)
- Commodities: dish, laundry, or bath soap; shampoo; toothpaste; toilet paper; Kleenex

Operating a Food Ministry

Most food pantries have a regular volunteer or part-time paid staff person available to coordinate the operation during the hours it is open. Volunteers should be on hand to sort the food and put it in bags for distribution. Keep in mind that you will not be able to meet the needs of everyone who comes to you for help. Therefore, this ministry should first meet the needs of the congregation, then needs in the community.

Most pantries have a policy of accepting referrals from their church's benevolence committee or from community social services. Those who are referred by the benevolence committee should already have the need ascertained. Those referred by the community are usually helped but referred to the benevolence committee to provide further assistance.

The primary function of the Food Ministry is not to feed people. It is to build a relationship with someone in need to present the gospel and to bring him or her into fellowship with believers. The coordinator or a designated volunteer should meet individually with the person or family to assess the need. Therefore, it is helpful to have volunteers who are willing to spend a little time with each person receiving food.

Some food ministries include preparing and serving hot meals. Much of this food may be contributed by area businesses or bought with donation certificates from area markets. This will take additional time, volunteers, and coordination to plan this type of event.

Holiday Food Drives and Distribution

Even ministries without food pantries make holiday food delivery a common practice, and it is a great idea when done correctly. Sometimes they assume a need without checking first. It is less embarrassing and more of a blessing to find out whether there really is a need before distributing baskets to anyone. We've seen families receive two or three baskets from different departments or ministries within the same church!

Again, start with those inside the church. Ask people who are elderly, handicapped, or single parents if they would like to receive a basket. Then include those you minister to outside the church.

A church in Ohio serves a hot meal at the church, and volunteers eat together and then deliver hot meals to shut-ins on Christmas and Thanksgiving. Single adults, single parents, and families share a holiday meal with friends and serve others at the same time.

Sample Questionnaire for Benevolence to Strangers or Transients

1. Do you attend a church locally? If so, did your church offer you assistance?

2. Where is your church, and what is your minister's name?

3. Have you sought assistance from any other churches in this area?

4. Do you have relatives who can assist you with your needs?

5. How were you referred to us?

6. What is your immediate need? (Please be specific.)

7. Are you receiving any aid from the government (un-employment, Social Security, food stamps, worker's comp)?

8. Have you worked a job or looked for work locally? When and where?

9. Are there any obstacles that hinder you from taking a job (child care, disability)?

10. Are you willing to work today if we know of an available job?

11. If we are unable to help you, what other options do you have?

12. If we are able to help you, how many people are involved? (Please list family members.)

13. Do you have some form of identification?

14. If you live in the area and your need is ongoing, are you willing to submit to financial and spiritual coaching?

Note: The local church should be aware of the validity of requests from its members and attendees through established relationships and small group accountability. However, questions 4, 6, 7, 8, 9, 10, and 14 should be examined if information is not known.

ENDNOTE

(Original questionnaire by Dave Pollack, Resource Ministries. Updated and revised June 1996.)

Your Response

Action Steps _____

_____

_____

_____

_____

_____

_____

_____

_____

_____

_____

_____

_____

Celebration Plan _____

_____

_____

_____

_____

_____

GIVING AND GENEROSITY

INTRODUCTION TO CHRIST

As important as our financial welfare is, it is not our highest priority. The single most important need of every person everywhere is to know God and experience the gift of His forgiveness and peace.

These five biblical truths will show you God's open door through a personal relationship with Jesus Christ.

1. God loves you and wants you to know Him and experience a meaningful life.

God created people in His own image, and He desires a close relationship with each of us. *"For God so loved the world, that He gave His only begotten Son, that whoever believes in Him shall not perish, but have eternal life"* (John 3:16). *"I [Jesus] came that they might have life, and have it abundantly"* (John 10:10).

God the Father loved you so much that He gave His only Son, Jesus Christ, to die for you.

2. Unfortunately, we are separated from God.

Because God is holy and perfect, no sin can abide in His presence. Every person has sinned, and the consequence of sin is separation from God. *"All have sinned and fall short of the glory of God"* (Romans 3:23). *"Your sins have cut you off from God"* (Isaiah 59:2, TLB).

3. God's only provision to bridge this gap is Jesus Christ.

Jesus Christ died on the cross to pay the penalty for our sin, bridging the gap between God and us. Jesus said, *"I am the way, and the truth, and the life; no one comes to the Father but through Me"* (John 14:6). *"God demonstrates His own love towards us, in that while we were yet sinners, Christ died for us"* (Romans 5:8).

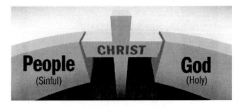

4. This relationship is a gift from God.

Our efforts can never achieve the perfection God requires. The only solution was to provide it to us as a gift.

When Jesus bore our sins on the cross, paying our penalty forever, He exchanged His righteousness for our guilt. By faith, we receive the gift we could never deserve.

Is that fair? Of course not! God's love exceeds His justice, resulting in mercy and grace toward us.

"It is by grace you have been saved, through faith— and this is not from yourselves, it is the gift of God— not by works, so that no one can boast" (Ephesians 2:8-9, NIV).

5. We must each receive Jesus Christ individually.

Someone has said that God has no grandchildren. Each of us is responsible before God for our own sin. We can continue to bear the responsibility and pay the consequences or we can receive the gift of Jesus' righteousness, enabling God to declare us "Not guilty!"

If you desire to know the Lord and are not certain whether you have this relationship, we encourage you to receive Christ right now. Pray a prayer similar to this suggested one:

> *"God, I need You. I invite Jesus to come into my life as my Savior and Lord and to make me the person You want me to be. Thank You for forgiving my sins and for giving me the gift of eternal life."*

You may be successful in avoiding financial quicksand—and we pray you will be—but without a relationship with Christ, it won't have lasting value. Eternal perspective begins with Him.

If you ask Christ into your life, please tell some people you know who are also following Christ. They will encourage you and help you get involved in a Bible-teaching church where you can grow spiritually. And please let us know as well. We would love to help in any way we can.

GOD'S OWNERSHIP & FINANCIAL FAITHFULNESS

How we view God determines how we live. Viewing Him as Savior is a good beginning, but growth comes when we view Him as Lord.

After losing his children and all his possessions, Job continued to worship God because he knew God was the Lord of those possessions and retained the ultimate rights over them. Realizing that God owed him nothing and he owed God everything enabled him to submit to God's authority and find contentment.

Moses walked away from his earthly inheritance, regarding *"disgrace for the sake of Christ as of greater value than the treasures of Egypt"* because he had his eye on God's reward (Hebrews 11:26, NIV).

Our willingness, like theirs, to give up a lesser value for a greater one, requires recognizing what most of the world does not: God is not only the Creator and Owner of all but also the ultimate definer of value. Those responsibilities belong to Him. He has retained them because He alone is capable of handling them.

Most of the frustration we experience in handling money comes when we take God's responsibilities on our own shoulders. Successful money management requires us to understand three aspects of God's Lordship—three roles for which He retains responsibility.

1. GOD OWNS IT ALL.

God owns all our possessions. *"To the Lord your God belong . . . the earth and everything in it"* (Deuteronomy 10:14, NIV). *"The earth is the Lord's, and all it contains"* (Psalm 24:1).

Leviticus 25:23 identifies Him as the owner of all the land: *"The land . . . shall not be sold permanently, for the land is Mine."* Haggai 2:8 says that He owns the precious metals: *"'The silver is Mine and the gold is Mine,' declares the Lord of hosts."*

Even our body—the one thing for which we would tend to claim total ownership—is not our own. *"Or do you not know that your body is a temple of the Holy Spirit who is in you, whom you have from God, and that you are not your own?"* (1 Corinthians 6:19).

The Lord created all things, and He never transferred the ownership of His creation to people. In Colossians 1:17 we are told that, *"In Him all things hold together."* At this very moment the Lord holds everything together by His power. As we will see throughout this study, recognizing God's ownership is crucial in allowing Jesus Christ to become the Lord of our money and possessions.

• Yielding Our Ownership to His Lordship

If we are to be genuine followers of Christ, we must transfer ownership of our possessions to Him. *"None of you can be My disciple who does not give up all his own possessions"* (Luke 14:33). Sometimes He tests us by asking us to give up the very possessions that are most important to us.

The most vivid example of this in Scripture is when God instructed Abraham, *"Take now your son, your only son, whom you love, Isaac . . . and offer him there as a burnt offering"* (Genesis 22:2). When Abraham obeyed, demonstrating his willingness to give up his most valuable possession, God responded, *"Do not lay a hand on the boy . . . now I know that you fear God, because you have not withheld from Me your son"* (Genesis 22:12, NIV).

When we acknowledge God's ownership, every spending decision becomes a spiritual decision. No longer do we ask, "Lord, what do You want me to do with my money?" It becomes, "Lord, what do You want me to do with Your money?" When we have this attitude and handle His money according to His wishes, spending and saving decisions become as spiritual as giving decisions.

• Recognizing God's Ownership

Our culture—the media, even the law—says that what you possess, you own. Acknowledging God's ownership requires a transformation of thinking, and this can be difficult. Many people say that God owns it all while they cling desperately to possessions that they think define them.

Here are a number of practical suggestions to help us recognize God's ownership.

- For the next 30 days, meditate on 1 Chronicles 29:11-12 when you first awake and just before going to sleep.

- For the next 30 days, ask God to make you aware of His ownership and help you to be thankful for it.

- Establish the habit of acknowledging God's ownership every time you buy something.

Recognizing God's ownership is important in learning contentment. When you believe you own something, you are more vulnerable to its circumstances. If it suffers loss or damage, your attitude can swing quickly from happy to discontented.

Recognizing it as God's loss doesn't make it irrelevant, but it does change your perspective. Now you can focus on how He will use this incident in causing *"all things to work together for good to those who love God, to those who are called according to His purpose"* (Romans 8:28).

2. GOD CONTROLS IT ALL.

Besides being Creator and Owner, God is ultimately in control of every event that occurs upon the earth. *"We adore you*

as being in control of everything"
(1 Chronicles 29:11, TLB). *"What-*
ever the Lord pleases, He does, in
heaven and in earth" (Psalm 135:6).
And in the book of Daniel, King Nebu-
chadnezzar stated: *"I praised the Most*
High; I honored and glorified him who lives
forever. . . . He does as he pleases with the pow-
ers of heaven and the peoples of the earth. No one
can hold back his hand or say to him: 'What have you
done?'" (Daniel 4:34-35, NIV).

God is also in control of difficult events. *"I am the Lord,*
and there is no other, the One forming light and creat-
ing darkness, causing well-being and creating calamity;
I am the Lord who does all these" (Isaiah 45:6-7).

It is important for us to realize that our heavenly Father
uses even seemingly devastating circumstances for
ultimate good in the lives of the godly. *"We know that*
God causes all things to work together for good to
those who love God, to those who are called accord-
ing to His purpose" (Romans 8:28). God allows difficult
circumstances for three reasons.

• He accomplishes His intentions.

This is illustrated in the life of Joseph, who was sold
into slavery as a teenager by his jealous brothers.
Joseph later said to his brothers: *"Do not be distressed*
and do not be angry with yourselves for selling me
here, because it was to save lives that God sent me
ahead of you. . . . It was not you who sent me here,
but God. . . . You intended to harm me, but God

intended it for good to accomplish what is now being done, the saving of many lives" (Genesis 45:5, 8; 50:20, NIV).

• He develops our character.

Godly character, something that is precious in His sight, is often developed during trying times. *"We also rejoice in our sufferings, because we know that suffering produces perseverance; perseverance, character"* (Romans 5:3-4, NIV).

• He disciplines His children.

"Those whom the Lord loves He disciplines. . . . He disciplines us for our good, so that we may share His holiness. All discipline for the moment seems not to be joyful, but sorrowful; yet to those who have been trained by it, afterwards it yields the peaceful fruit of righteousness" (Hebrews 12:6,10-11).

When we are disobedient, we can expect our loving Lord to discipline us, often through difficult circumstances. His purpose is to encourage us to abandon our sin and to "share His holiness."

You can be at peace knowing that your loving heavenly Father is in control of every situation you will ever face. He will use every one of them for a good purpose.

3. GOD PROVIDES IT ALL.

God promises to provide our needs. *"But seek first His kingdom and His righteousness, and all these things [food and*

clothing] will be added to you"
(Matthew 6:33).

The same God who fed manna to
the children of Israel during their 40
years of wandering in the wilderness
and who fed 5,000 with only five loaves
and two fish has promised to provide our
needs. This is the same God who told Elijah,
*"I have commanded the ravens to provide for you
there. . . . The ravens brought him bread and meat
in the morning and bread and meat in the evening"*
(1 Kings 17:4, 6).

God—Both Predictable and Unpredictable

God is totally predictable in His faithfulness to provide for our
needs. What we cannot predict is how He will provide. He uses
various and often surprising means—an increase in income or
a gift. He may provide an opportunity to stretch limited resources through money-saving purchases. Regardless of how He
chooses to provide for our needs, He is completely reliable.

Our culture believes that God plays no part in financial matters; they assume that His invisibility means He is uninvolved.
They try to shoulder responsibilities that God never intended
for them—burdens of ownership, control, and provision that
only He can carry.

Jesus said, *"Come to Me, all who are weary and heavy-laden,
and I will give you rest. Take My yoke upon you. . . . For My
yoke is easy, and My burden is light"* (Matthew 11:28-30). This
is the only way we can rest and enjoy the peace of God.

When we trust God to do His part in our finances, we can focus on doing our part: being financially faithful with every resource He has given us.

Defining Financial Faithfulness

Faithfully living by God's financial principles doesn't necessarily mean having a pile of money in the bank, but it does bring an end to overdue bills and their related stress. And that's not the most important part; that's just relief from symptoms.

Consider some of the big-picture benefits:

- Assurance that God is in control of our circumstances
- Absolute faith in His promise to meet all of our needs
- A clear conscience before God
- A clear conscience with others

This is not to say that we will live on financial autopilot with no more challenges for the rest of our lives. God promises no such thing. In fact, without challenges our faith has no opportunity to be perfected or even to grow; without challenges it isn't active or visible. But peace in the midst of challenges is a miraculous quality of life, and that's what God promises when we learn to trust and follow Him fully.

With God in control, we have nothing to fear. He is the Master of the universe. His wisdom is superior to ours in every way, and no situation is too complex or hopeless for Him to solve.

God has even provided a solution for our ongoing frailties and failings. As part of His great redemption, He offers continuing forgiveness and cleansing from all unrighteousness (1 John 1:9). We make mistakes—sometimes willfully violating His plan for us—but He welcomes our confession and honors it by restoring our fellowship and renewing our guidance.

Once we begin to experience the rewards of financial faithfulness, we never want to be without them. Our deepening trust in *God's* faithfulness intensifies our desire to stay within His will, resulting in perfect peace.

Many people have inherited or achieved financial independence: a level of wealth that requires no further work or income. But apart from Christ, they don't have freedom from anxiety; they have merely replaced one set of worries with another. They often fear:

- Loss of what they have accumulated
- Loss of meaningful relationships—fearing that others only care about what they have rather than who they are
- Loss of safety as their wealth makes them a target for theft or kidnapping
- Loss of grace from others, who jealously hold them to a higher standard because of their wealth

Being financially free, on the other hand, includes freedom from these fears as well as from the oppression of envy, covetousness, and greed.

Financial faithfulness is transformation—a process that requires God's power and our participation. It is synonymous with our definition of true financial faithfulness in the *Crown Money Map™*:

1. Knowing that God owns it all.

2. Finding contentment with what He provides.

3. Being free to be all He made you to be.

This is the big picture, the framework within which wealth and material possessions take their rightful place—not as ends but as means—in God's hands.

Steps to Cultivate Financial Faithfulness

Now it is time to outline the path. Since we're talking about transformation, you'll notice that some of our steps go well beyond mere money-management techniques.

1. TRANSFER OWNERSHIP.

Transferring ownership of every possession to God means acknowledging that He already owns them and that we will begin treating them accordingly. This includes more than just material possessions; it includes money, time, family, education, even earning potential for the future. This is essential to experience the Spirit-filled life in the area of finances (see Psalm 8:4-6).

There is no substitute for this step. If we believe we are the owners of even a single possession, then the events affecting that possession are going to affect our attitudes. God will not input His perfect will into our lives unless we first surrender our wills to Him.

However, if we make a total transfer of everything to God, He will demonstrate His ability. It is important to understand and accept God's conditions for His control (see Deuteronomy 5:32-33). God will keep His promise to provide our every need according to His perfect plan.

It is easy to say we will make a total transfer of everything to God, but it's not so easy to do. Our desire for control and our habit of self-management cause difficulty in consistently seeking God's will in the area of material things. But without a deep conviction that He is in control, we can never experience true financial faithfulness.

What a great relief it is to turn our burdens over to Him. Then, if something happens to the car, we can say, "Father, I gave this car to You; I've maintained it to the best of my ability, but I don't own it. It belongs to You, so do with it whatever You like." Then look for the blessing God has in store as a result of this attitude.

2. BECOME DEBT FREE.

God wants us to be free to serve Him without restriction. *"You were bought with a price; do not become slaves of men"* (1 Corinthians 7:23). *"The rich rules over the poor, and the borrower becomes the lender's slave"* (Proverbs 22:7).

Read *Debt and Bankruptcy*, another book in the *MoneyLife™ Basics Series*, for further information on this, including definitions and steps for getting out of debt. For most, this will involve sacrifice—at least initially—but the payoff is well worth it.

3. GIVE REGULARLY AND GENEROUSLY.

Every follower of Christ should establish tithing (10 percent of income) as a beginning point of giving and as a testimony to God's ownership. We can't say we have given total ownership to God if our actions don't back the claim.

It is through sharing that we bring His power in finances into focus. In every case, God wants us to give the first part to Him, but He also wants us to pay our creditors. This requires establishing a plan, and it will probably mean making sacrifices of wants and desires until all obligations are current.

We cannot sacrifice God's part—that is not our prerogative as faithful, obedient followers of Christ. Malachi 3:8-9 has strong words for those who "rob God." But then verses 10-12 describe His great blessing for those who tithe fully.

God, as the first giver, wants us to be like Him, and His economy rewards our generosity. *"Now this I say, he who sows sparingly will also reap sparingly, and he who sows bountifully will also reap bountifully"* (2 Corinthians 9:6).

Steps two and three combine to form an important conclusion. If, while en route to financial faithfulness, sacrifice becomes necessary—and it almost always does—our sacrifice must not come from God's or our creditor's share. We must choose areas within our other discretionary expenses to sacrifice. Consider it an opportunity to exercise faith in God's reward for our obedience.

4. ACCEPT GOD'S PROVISION.

To obtain financial peace, recognize and accept that God's provision is used to direct each of our lives. Often Christians lose sight of the fact that God's will can be accomplished through a withholding of funds; we think that He can direct us only by an abundance of money. But God does not choose for everyone to live in great abundance. This does not imply poverty, but it may mean that God wants us to be more responsive to His day-by-day control.

Followers of Christ must learn to live on what God provides and not give in to a driving desire for wealth or the pressure brought on by comparison with others. This necessitates planning our lifestyle within the provision God has supplied. When we are content to do this, God will always help us find a way.

5. KEEP A CLEAR CONSCIENCE.

Living with integrity means dealing with the past as well as the present. Part of becoming financially faithful requires gaining a clear conscience regarding past business practices and personal dealings. Sometimes, in addition to a changed attitude, our transformation means making restitution for situations where we have wronged someone.

Tim's story is a good example. Before he accepted Christ, he cheated someone out of some money. God convicted him about this and indicated that he should go and make restitution. He contacted the person, confessed what had been done, and offered to make it right. The person refused to forgive and also refused to take any money.

Tim's ego and pride were hurt until he realized that he had been both obedient and successful. His confession was not primarily for the offended person but for his own relationship with God. He had done exactly what God had asked, and God had forgiven him. Nothing further was required.

6. PUT OTHERS FIRST.

This does not imply being a door mat; it simply means that we shouldn't profit at the unfair expense of someone else. As is often the case, attitude is all-important.

7. MANAGE TIME PRIORITIES.

A workaholic might gain wealth at the expense of the family's relational needs, but wealth alone is no indicator of financial faithfulness. And wealth gained with wrong priorities is likely to vanish. *"Do not weary yourself to gain wealth, cease from your consideration of it. When you set your eyes on it, it is gone. For wealth certainly makes itself wings like an eagle that flies toward the heavens"* (Proverbs 23:4-5). Even if it doesn't vanish, it can't deliver the satisfaction it promises. Don't be deceived by overcommitment to business or the pursuit of wealth.

God's priorities for us are very clear.

Priority number one is to develop our relationship with Jesus Christ.

Priority number two is our family. This includes teaching them God's Word. And that requires quality time, something that can't exist without a sufficient quantity from which to flow.

Develop the habit of a regular time to study God's Word for yourself as well as a family time that acknowledges your commitment to each other and to God.

Turn off the television, have the children do their homework early, and begin to study the Bible together. Pray for each other and for those in need. Help your children become intercessors who can pray for others and expect God to answer.

Priority number three is your work, which God intends to be an opportunity for ministry and personal development in addition to providing an income.

Priority number four is church activities and other ministry. This does not imply that it is unimportant or can be neglected, but it keeps us from using church as an excuse to let higher priorities slide. If we observe priority number one, we will not neglect our church.

8. AVOID OVER-INDULGENCE.

Jesus said, *"If anyone wishes to come after Me, he must deny himself, and take up his cross daily and follow Me"* (Luke 9:23). Once again, this is about priorities. Who wins the contest between God's claim on your life and your own pursuit of pleasure?

In Philippians 3:18-19, Paul says that many live as the enemies of the cross of Christ, and he describes them by saying, *"Their destiny is destruction, their god is their stomach, and their glory is in their shame"* (NIV).

That sounds alarmingly like much of our culture, and it takes great effort to avoid being swept along with the current.

9. GET CHRISTIAN COUNSEL.

"Without consultation, plans are frustrated, but with many counselors they succeed" (Proverbs 15:22). God admonishes us to seek counsel and not to rely solely on our own resources. People are often frustrated in financial planning because they lack the necessary knowledge. A common but tragic response is to give up. Within the body of Christ, God has supplied those who have the ability to help in the area of finances. Seek Christian counselors.

To read more on what God says about handling money, go to Crown.org and click "Bible Tools."

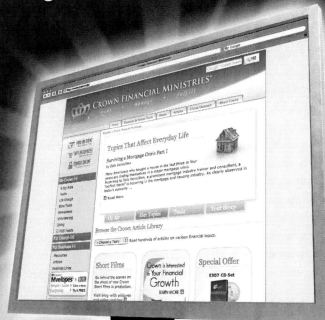

CROWN FINANCIAL MINISTRIES

Crown Financial Ministries® is an interdenominational Christian organization dedicated to equipping people around the world to learn, apply and teach biblical financial principles. Since 1976, Crown has taught or equipped more than 50 million people with the life-transforming message of faithfully living by God's financial principles in every area of their lives.

Through the generosity of donors and volunteers around the globe, Crown serves the followers of Christ worldwide, ranging from those entrusted with wealth to those living in desperate poverty. Regardless of their economic status, we rejoice with believers who develop a more intimate relationship with Jesus Christ, become free to serve Him, and more generously fund the Great Commission.

For volunteer, short-term missions, or giving opportunities with Crown, visit us online at Crown.org or call 1-800-722-1976.

MoneyLife **BASICS SERIES BOOK**

Pocket-Sized Help and Hope

INVESTING
AND
INSURANCE

[Insurance]
[Investing]

MONEYLIFE™ BASICS SERIES

ISBN 978-1-56427-253-9

◀ Learn the foundational basics of
investing and insurance

SPENDING
PLAN
SOLUTIONS

[Spending Plan/Budgeting]
Major Purchases-Houses and Cars

MONEYLIFE™ BASICS SERIES

ISBN 978-1-56427-252-2

DEBT AND
BANKRUPTCY

[Debt and Credit]
Bankruptcy
Gambling/Lotteries

MONEYLIFE™ BASICS SERIES

ISBN 978-1-56427-251-5

▲ Create a successful spending plan,
and plan for major purchases like
homes and automobiles

◀ Understand the pitfalls of debt, the
ins and outs of bankruptcy, and
the dangers of gambling

Resources

To Help You in Life and Money

Career Direct®

You have unlimited potential to be more, do more, and maximize your God-given talents and abilities. You are ready to exceed everyone's expectations.

Go to CareerDirectOnline.org to get started.

Crown Budgeting Solutions

Choose the Budgeting Solution That Fits Your Lifestyle

Paper
• Traditional option using paper, pen, and cash.

Software
• Computer software option for your PC or Mac.

Online and Mobile
• Web and Mobile option available anytime, anywhere.